Virginia Heraldica

Virginia Heraldica

Being a Registry of Virginia Gentry Entitled to Coat Armor

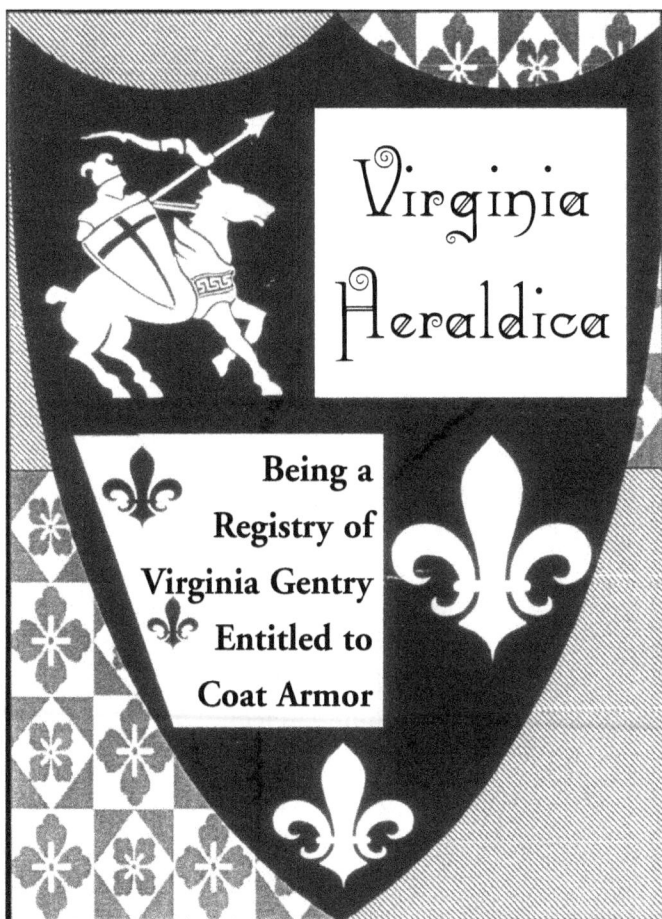

with Genealogical Notes of the Families

Edited by

William Armstrong Crozier

HERITAGE BOOKS
2008

HERITAGE BOOKS

AN IMPRINT OF HERITAGE BOOKS, INC.

Books, CDs, and more—Worldwide

For our listing of thousands of titles see our website
at
www.HeritageBooks.com

A Facsimile Reprint
Published 2008 by
HERITAGE BOOKS, INC.
Publishing Division
100 Railroad Ave. #104
Westminster, Maryland 21157

Originally published
New York
1908

International Standard Book Numbers
Paperbound: 978-0-7884-1920-1
Clothbound: 978-0-7884-7456-9

Virginia Heraldica

ADAMS. New Kent county.

Arms: Ermine three cats passant in pale azure.

Ebenezar Adams, gent., of St. Peter's parish, New Kent, was in Va. ante. 1714; died 13 June, 1735. He was the son of Richard Adams of Abridge, Essex, Eng., citizen and merchant tailor of London, and his wife Anne. From her will which is filed in the Preg. Court of Canterbury, London, 8 Oct., 1734, she styles herself widow. Ebenezar Adams, married about 1718, Tabitha, dau. of Richard Cocke of Bremo, Va. Their sixth child, Thomas Adams, born about 1730 in New Kent, died 1788 in Augusta county, used on his seal the arms of Adams of London, a branch of the county Salop family.

ALLEN. Surry county.

Arms: Per chevron gules and ermine, in chief two lions' heads erased or.

Crest: A horse's head.

Arthur Allen, the immigrant, born 1602, died 1670; patented 200 acres in 1649, between Lawnes and Lower Chippoakes Creeks. He built the house known as "Bacons Castle." His wife was Alice, sister of Daniel Tucker of York county. Their son, Major Arthur Allen, Speaker of the House of Burgesses, married Katherine, daughter of Captain Lawrence Baker of Surry county. The will of Arthur 2nd was proved in Surry, 5 Sept., 1710. He had issue, Elizabeth, John, Katherine, James, Arthur, Ann, Mary, and Joseph Allen. The son John Allen, will proved 5 March, 1741, married Elizabeth, born 1697, died 1738, daughter of William Bassett, of the Council of Va. Upon Elizabeth Allen's tombstone at Claremont, Surry, are found the arms of Allen, impaling Bassett, the latter being," argent, three bars wavy gules.

The arms of the Virginia family are the same as those of the Derbyshire, Staffordshire and London families, with the exception of the crest, which in the English arms has the "horse's head issuing from a ducal coronet."

BRAY. James City county.

Arms: Azure a chevron between three eagles legs erased a la Cuisse sable, armed gules.

Crest: An ounce ppr.

James Bray, J. P., of James City county 1666; member of the Council, 4 March, 1674-5; married Angelica ———. They had issue, (1) Thomas; (2) James, J. P., of James City county, in 1710, vestryman of Bruton parish; sheriff in 1717; married about 1698, Mourning, widow of Col. Thomas Pettus. (3) Col. David Bray, J. P., of James City county, 1710; vestryman of Bruton parish; had issue David, born 1699, member of the Council; died 1731; married Elizabeth, dau. of John Page of Gloucester. (4) Angelica, married Mingo Inglis of Williamsburg. The Bray arms are on the tombs of the first and second David Bray in Bruton churchyard. They correspond with the arms of Bray in the Visitation of Nottingham in 1614.

JETT. King George county.

Arms: Argent three fleurs de lis.

At the court house at Williamsburg is a letter of Thomas Jett of Rappahannock River, dated 28 Oct., 1774, sealed with above arms, and addressed to Mrs. Dorothy Jordan. Thomas Jett had a son William Storke Jett, and two brothers who resided in King George county, viz: Francis Jett, whose will was proved in 1761, and whose wife was Frances ———; and Burkett Jett, whose will was proved in 1771.

The arms of Jett of London are, "Argent on a cross gules, five fleurs de lis of the field." There is no cross in the Virginia arms.

KEEBLE. Middlesex county.

Arms: Argent a chevron engrailed gules, on a chief azure three escallops of the field.

Crest: An elephant's head couped.

From a wax impression on a deed at Urbana, Middlesex, dated 1698, and signed by George Keeble.

These arms are somewhat similar to those of Sir Henry Keble, Knt. temp. Henry VIII., whose dau. Alice married William Browne, son and heir to Sir John Browne, Knt., Lord Mayor of London. (See Visitation of London, 1568.)

ENGLISH. Lancaster county.

Arms: Four martlets, three and one.

Will of Alexander English, dated 23 Jan., 1685, prob. 10 March, 1696, Lancaster. He mentions his brother Mr. William English in England. The will is sealed with a wax impression bearing the above arms.

The will of another Alexander English in same county, dated 16 Dec., 1696, prob. 14 Apl., 1697, leaves a small estate to Joseph, son of William and Susana Paine. This will is sealed with a duplicate of the above arms, so that it is evident there was some degree of relationship between them. There are, however, no arms given in the English records in the name of English, which have four birds as charges.

ABRAHALL. New Kent county.

Arms: Azure three hedgehogs or.

Crest: A hedgehog ppr

Wax seal on a deed dated 1690, from Colonel Robert Abrahall of New Kent to William Bassett.

The arms are similar to those of Abrahall of the county of Herefordshire.

CAY. Elizabeth City county.

Crest: A hawk.

The above crest is on a bookplate in a book entitled, "Johnstons Edition of Shakespeare," and was once the property of Gabriel Cay, one of the Justices of Elizabeth City county, in 1767. The English authorities give for Cay, "A hand ppr. and flotant behind, a pennon vert, tied round the neck and charged with the arms. Cay of Northumberland use "a royal eagle," and Cay of Durham "a griffin's head."

GARLICK.

Arms: Argent three heads of garlick ppr.

The above arms of Edward Garlick of Va. are engraved on an old silver bowl, now the property of Mrs. John B. Minor.

LANGBORNE. King William county.

Arms: Argent two chevrons gules.

Arms on the tomb of William Langborne in King William county. He was born in 1723, and was the son of Robert Langborne of Fetter Lane, London, and his wife Mary Dandridge. The tomb also bears the arms of his mother, viz: "Azure a lion's head erased or, between three mascles argent." He married Susannah Smith of Shooters Hill, by whom he had Colonel William Langborne of the Revolution.

AITCHISON. Princess Anne county.

Arms: A double-headed eagle displayed.

Upon the tomb of William Aitchison at Rose Hall, Princess Anne county, are the above arms, nearly obliterated. His will was probated 12 June, 1777. The various Aitchison families of Scotland bear the above charge in their arms, with the addition of other charges. Some portions of the shield have become defaced, so that it is impossible to say to what branch the above William belonged.

FOX. Gloucester county.

Arms: Argent a chevron sable, between three cocks gules, on a chief azure a fox courant or.

Crest: A lion sejant guardant or, supporting with the dexter foot a book of the last.

Arms engraved on the tomb of Isabel Fox, wife of the Reverend John Fox, minister of Ware parish, and daughter of Mr. Thomas Booth. She died 13 June, 1742, aged 38 years.

These are the arms of Fox of Missenden, Buckinghamshire.

ANDREWS. Williamsburg.

Arms: Azure a cross ermine, between four fleurs de lis or.

Robert Andrews, son of Moses and Letitia (Cooke) Andrews, and great-grandson of John Andrews, who came from Leicestershire to Maryland in 1654, and who was descended from Anthony Andrews of Bisbrooke, county of Rutland. Robert Andrews was born in Penna. and was tutor in the family of Mann Page. He was Professor in Wiliam and Mary College in 1779, and private secretary in 1781 to General Nelson at Yorktown. He represented Williamsburg in 1788 at the State convention, and was member of the Legislature in 1798. He married first, Elizabeth Ballard, and secondly, Mary Blair.

BATCHELDOR. Middlesex county.

Arms: A double-headed eagle displayed.

Upon a wax seal on the will of John Batcheldor, 1685, at Urbanna. He is probably the John Batcheldor who embarked for St. Christophers, 2 Oct., 1635, on the "John" of London, at which time he was aged 26 years. (Hotten.)

In the Christ Church, Middlesex, parish register we find the following entry: "Mr. John Batcheldor departed this life 4 Xemb. and was buried at home the 15 Xemb., 1685. In the same register we find, Mary, dau. of John and Mary Batcheldor, bapt. 12 Sept., 1653; Sarah, dau. of above, born ———; Rebecca, dau. of above, born 2 Oct., 1658; William, son of above, born 22 July, 1667.

The British authorities give no such arms as above in the name of Batcheldor.

GORDON. Dinwiddie county.

Arms: Azure three boars heads erased or.

Arms on tomb in Blandford churchyard of Samuel Gordon, son of David Gordon, Esq., of Craig, county Kirkcudbright. Died 14 April, 1771, aged 54 years.

LUDWELL. Williamsburg.

Arms: Gules on a bend argent between two towers or, three eagles displayed sable.

Motto: I pensieri stretti edil viso sciolto.

Thomas Ludwell came to Virginia about 1642, and was Secretary of the Colony in 1660. He was a son of Thomas Ludwell of Bruton, Somersetshire, and Jane, daughter of James Cottington, the brother of Lord Cottington. He died 1 Oct., 1678, but left no issue.

Philip Ludwell was brother of Thomas and was Deputy-Secretary 1675-77, he was also Governor of North Carolina and member of the Va. Council. He married, 1st, Lucy, daughter of Captain Robert Higginson, and, 2nd, Frances Berkeley, widow of Sir William Berkeley. He left issue by his first marriage, and died in England about 1707. The above arms are on a book plate, dated 1737, of Philip Ludwell of Green Spring in Va., Esq.

ASHTON. Northumberland county.

Arms: Argent a mullet sable.

Charles Ashton was a resident of Northumberland county in 1660; Justice of the Peace and Captain in the Militia. He died in 1672. His grandson, Colonel Henry Ashton, was born in 1671, and died in 1731, and upon his tombstone on Nominy Creek is engraved the above arms, which are the same as Ashton of Chadderton in the county of Lancashire. The immigrant is thought to have been descended from the Ashtons of Spalding, Lincolnshire, a branch of the Chadderton family.

BAKER. Norfolk.

Arms: Argent on a fess nebulee between three keys sable, a tower triple towered of the first.

Wax seal on a deed of Henry Baker, now in possession of Richard H. Baker, Esq., of Norfolk. The arms are those of Baker of Kent.

EVELYN. James City county.

Arms: Azure a griffin passant and a chief or.

Crest: A griffin passant or, beaked, forelegged and ducally gorged azure.

Motto: Durete.

Robert Evelyn, son of Robert Evelyn of Long Ditton and Godstone, county of Surrey (an uncle of John Evelyn, the Diarist), was born in 1606. He came to Virginia in 1634, and in 1637 was Surveyor-General and member of the Council. He returned to England, but afterwards became a resident of Maryland, being Commander of Kent Isle, and member of the Assembly 1637-38, and 1642.

Captain George Evelyn, brother of Robert, was born in 1609, and resided in James City county. He had two children, Mountjoy, who married into the Robins family of Northampton county, and a daughter Rebecca, who married, first, Bartholomew Knipe of Virginia and, secondly (prior to 1658), Colonel Daniel Parke, Snr., by whom she has left many descendants.

BARRADALL. Williamsburg.

Arms: A bend between three pheons, an annulet for difference.

In Bruton Churchyard, Williamsburg, is the tomb of Edward Barradall, Attorney-General of Virginia, who died 1743. Upon it are the arms as above, impaling Fitzhugh, viz., "Azure three chevrons brased in base, interlaced or, a chief of the last." Edward Barradall married Sarah, daughter of Colonel William Fitzhugh. No tinctures can be distinguished on the Attorney-General's arms. The arms given by Burke to Barradall or Borrodaile, are, "Or three water bougets in pale sable, between two torteaux a chief vert."

BASKERVILLE. York county.

Arms: Argent a chevron gules between three hurts.

Crest: A forester vested vert, edged or, holding over his dexter shoulder a crossbow of the last, and with the other hand in a leash, a hound passant argent.

John Baskerville was in York county ante 1667, and was Clerk of the Court. He died in 1675. Married Mary, daughter of Lt.-Col. William Barber of York. Issue: Mary and George, whose descendants settled in Cumberland county. The above John, born in 1635, was the 5th child of John Baskerville and Magdalen, his wife, of Goosetry, Cheshire, and was descended from John de Baskervyle, Knt., of Old Withington, A. D. 1266 (See Omerod's History of Cheshire). Henry Baskerville, the 6th child of John and Magdalen, was a citizen and Fishmonger of London, and his will, proved in Preg. Court of Canterbury, 19 May, 1676, mentions his brother John in Virginia.

FAUNTLEROY. Richmond county.

Arms: Gules three infant's heads crined or.

Crest: A fleur de lis or, between two wings expanded azure.

The first of this family in Virginia was Major Moore Fauntleroy, who was in the colony prior to 1648. He is believed to have been a son of John Fauntleroy, gent., of Crandall, county of Southampton. In 1633, Sir John Borough, Garter King of Arms, confirmed the above arms to Moore Fauntleroy, gent., who is thought to have been the immigrant. William Fauntleroy, either a son or grandson of Moore, was born in 1684 and died in 1757. He married Apphia Bushrod, and had issue: William, born 1713; Moore, born 1716, whose children moved to King and Queen county; and John, born 1724.

BATHURST. New Kent county.

Arms: Quarterly, 1st and 4th. Sable two bars ermined, in chief three crosses patee or. 2nd and 3rd. gules a chevron between three lances argent.

The immigrant was Lancelot Bathurst, who was in New Kent county in 1683. In 1688 he was clerk of the committee of Private Causes in House of Burgesses, and in 1698 served as High Sheriff of New Kent. He was the 5th son of Sir Edward Bathurst and his 2nd wife, Susan Rich, of Cranbrook, Kent. The name of his wife is unknown. He had issue, a daughter, who married prior to 1704, William Tomlin; Mary, who married prior to 1704, Francis Meriwether; Susan, married Drury Stith; Lawrence, who d.s.p. in Essex county. His will dated 29 Dec., 1704, prob. 11 Feb., 1705, mentions his above named sisters.

OFFLEY. Princess Anne county.

Arms: Argent on a cross pattee flory azure, a lion passant guardant or, between four Cornish choughs ppr.

Sara Offley, daughter of Robert Offley and Anne Osborne, was baptized at St. Benet's, London, 16 April, 1609; married 18 July, 1627, at St. Anne's, Blackfriars, to Adam Thorowgood, and died in Virginia in 1627. Her tomb at Church Point, Princess Anne county, has the above arms. The English pedigree of Offley is as follows:

(1) John Offley, of Staffordshire, married Margery. (2) William Offley, Mayor of Stafford in 1517, married twice. (3) Robert Offley, eldest son of the 2nd marriage, born at Chester, removed to London and was buried at St. Benet's, 29 April, 1596. (4) Robert Offley, married 3 Feb., 1588, to Anne Osborne; he died 16 May, 1625. Anne Osborne was the daughter of Sir Edward Osborne, Knt., Lord Mayor of London in 1585. (5) Sara Offley. wife of Adam Thorowgood, member of the Virginia Council in 1637.

LISTER. Lancaster county.
Arms: Azure on a cross argent, five torteaux, each charged with a mullet or.
Crest: A stag's head erased ppr.
Wax seal on the will of Edmund Lister. 1709, of Lancaster county.

BEALE. York county.
Arms: Sable on a chevron between three griffin's heads erased argent, three estoiles gules.
Crest: A unicorn's head erased or. semee of estoiles gules.
Arms on tomb of Captain Thomas Beale, Jr., at Chestnut Hill, Richmond county. He was born in 1649 and died 16 Oct., 1679. He married Ann, daughter of Colonel William Gooch of Temple Farm, York county, and by her had sons, Thomas and Charles, and two daughters. His father, Colonel Thomas Beale of York oounty, was a member of the Council under Governor Berkeley. The arms are identical with those of Beale of London.

REID. Middlesex county.
Arms: A chevron between three eagle's heads.
Crest: An eagle's head.
Upon the will of James Reid, merchant, Urbanna, 3 Jan., 1764, is the above seal, the tinctures, however, cannot be distinguished. He died without issue in America, leaving a legacy to his sister Jean Reid of Ayrshire, Scotland.

BERNARD. Gloucester county.
Arms: Argent a bear rampant sable, muzzled or.
Crest: A demi-bear muzzled and collared or.
Motto: Bear and forbear.
The first of this family in Virginia was Richard Bernard, gent., widower, aged 26 years, who obtained a marriage license, 24 Nov., 1634, to marry Anna Corderoy, aged 22 years, daughter of ———— Corderoy, Esq., at St. Andrew's in the Wardrobe, London. (Chester's London Marriage Licenses.) He was in the Colony 3 Jan., 1647, in which year he rented from Captain Thomas Harwood of Virginia and others, "the plantation in York oounty, called 'Pryor's Plantation,'" for a term of three years. To this deed is attached a rough drawing made by the Clerk of the Court, of a shield bearing the arms common to the Bernards of Buckingham. Richard Bernard was dead in 1652, as a deed recorded in York in 1662,

states that "Anna Bernard, now of Purton, in Petsoe parish, Gloucester, widow, purchased Pryor's Plantation in 1652 from Thomas Edwards of the Inner Temple, London, and Margaret, his wife, one of the daughters of William Pryor, decd. Anna Bernard had a son Richard, who was vestryman of Petsworth Parish in 1677, died 1691. He left sons, Philip and John Bernard.

SMITH. Abingdon, Gloucester county.

Arms: Azure a chevron between three acorns slipped and leaved or.

Major Lawrence Smith of Gloucester married Mary ————. His will was dated 8 Aug., 1700. His eldest son John was a member of the Council and died in Abingdon Parish about 1719. He married Elizabeth, daughter and heiress of Henry Cox of Rappahannock county and his wife Arabella, daughter of William Strachey of Gloucester, the grandson of William Strachey, who was Secretary to Lord Delaware in 1610. Lawrence, second son of Major Lawrence Smith, settled in York county and was Colonel, Justice, Sheriff and one of the feofees of Yorktown. He married 1st, Mildred, daughter of Captain Thomas Chisman, and 2nd, Mildred, daughter of John Reade. His granddaughter Mildred, daughter of his son Edmund Smith, married David Jameson, and the Jameson arms impaling Smith are found on her tomb at Temple Farm. (See Jameson arms.) The Smith arms are the same as Smith of Tottne, Devonshire.

BOOTH. Gloucester county.

Arms: Argent three boars' heads erect, erased sable.

Crest: A demi-St. Catherine ppr. couped at the knees, habited argent, crowned or; in the dexter hand a Catherine wheel, in the sinister a sword, point downward.

The immigrant, Thomas Booth, settled in Gloucester and is thought to have come from Lancashire, as the above arms are those of Booth of Barton, county Lancashire. They are found on the tomb of Mary Cooke, the wife of his grandson, Thomas Booth, on which they are impaled with Cooke. (See Cooke arms.)

ROBINSON. Middlesex county.

Arms: Vert on a chevron argent between three roebucks trippant or, as many trefoils slipped gules.

Crest: A roebuck trippant or.

Motto: Propere et provide.

Colonel Christopher Robinson of Middlesex, born 1645 at Cleasby, Yorkshire, was a son of John Robinson and Elizabeth, daughter of Christopher Potter of Cleasby. Another son was John Robinson, Bishop of London. Christopher Robinson was in Virginia in 1666, and settled in Middlesex, calling his estate "Hewick." He was a member of the Council and House of Burgesses in 1691; Secretary of State 1692, dying in the following year. He married 1st, Agatha, daughter of Bertram Obert, and 2nd, Catherine, widow of Major Robert Beverley.

NOTT. Williamsburg.

Arms: Azure on a bend between three leopards' faces or, as many martlets gules.

Crest: A martlet argent, ducally crowned or, in the beak an olive branch ppr.

The above arms are on the tomb of Edward Nott, Esq., Governor of Virginia, who died 23 August, 1706, aged 49 years, and whose remains are buried in Bruton Church.

The arms are the same as Nott of London and Kent.

BATT. York county.

Arms: Argent a chevron between three reremice displayed sable.

William Batt received a grant of 220 acres, 5 Sept., 1643, on Mobjack Bay; John Batt and John Davis, 750 acres in York county, 2 April, 1667; Thomas and Henry Batt, 5878 acres, 6 Aug., 1668, in Charles City.

The Virginia immigrants descend from the family of Batt of Okewell in the Wapentake of Agbrigg and Morley. In the Harleian MS. No. 4630, their pedigree is given as follows: Henry Batt of Okewell, living in the reigns of Henry VIII. to 2nd of Mary, purchased the manor of Burstall and others near Bradford-dale. Issue, Henry and John. Henry married a daughter of Richard Wilkinson of Bradford, and had issue, Henry, Robert and Richard. Robert, son of Henry Batt, was Fellow and Master of University College, Oxon, and married Mary, daughter of John Parry, of Golden Valley, Herts, and had issue, John, William and Henry. John, son of Robert above, married Martha, daughter of Thomas Mallory, Dean of Chester, and had issue, (1) John, drowned in the Irish sea coming from Virginia with his father; (2) William, (3) Thomas, (4) Henry, the last three in Virginia in 1667. William, son of John and Martha Batt, married Elizabeth, daughter of William Horton, and had issue, William, Gladdhill, John, Thomas, Elizabeth, Martha and Judith. John, son of William and Elizabeth, was living in 1702 and married a daughter of ———— Metcalf.

RANDOLPH. Henrico county.

Arms: Gules on a cross or, five mullets of the first.

Crest: An antelope's head couped, holding in its mouth a stick or.

The pedigree of the Virginia Randolphs is as follows: (1) Robert Randolph of Hams, Sussex. (2) William, born 1572, of Northamptonshire. (3) Richard, born 21 Feb., 1621, died in Dublin, 1671, married. Elizabeth, daughter of Richard Ryland of Warwickshire. (4) Richard, 2nd son of the last, born 1651, died 11 April, 1711. came to Virginia about 1660, and the 29 July, 1669, succeeded his uncle, Henry Randolph, as clerk of Henrico. Henry was born about 1623 and came to the colony in 1643. he was a member of the House of Burgesses, and married Judith, daughter of Henry Soane, Speaker of the House of Burgesses. William Randolph settled at Turkey Island, and was Justice of Henrico 1683-1711; Burgess 1685-99, and 1703-05, and again in 1710; Attorney-General in 1696; Speaker of the House of Burgesses 1698; Clerk of the House in 1702. He married Mary, daughter of Henry Isham of Bermuda Hundred, and left issue. At the Henrico Court House there is a paper dated 1698, which bears a wax impression of his arms. There is also a book plate of his descendant, Sir John Randolph, which bears the same arms.

CHAPMAN. Stafford county.

Arms: Per chevron argent and gules, in the centre a crescent counterchanged.

Crest: An arm embowed in armor, holding a broken spear encircled with a wreath.

Motto: Crescit sub pondere virtus.

In the will of Constantia Chapman, dated 2 Nov., 1768, filed at Stafford, is the following bequest: "I give and bequeath unto each of my three grandchildren, H. C. Weems, Wm. Locke Weems and Sarah Louisa Weems, the sum of five guineas to be laid out for them in silver plate, as their mother shall think proper, the said plate to be engraved with the arms of the Chapman and Pearson families." On a silver salver, now owned by Mrs. Susan Swann Calvert, of Alexandria, Va., the above combined arms are found, as follows: As above for Chapman, and for Pearson, "Per fess embattled azure and gules, three suns or." Constantia Chapman was daughter of Simon Pearson, gent., of Overwharton Parish, Stafford; his will was probated in 1733. (For Pearson family, see under that name.)

BICKLEY. Louisa county.

Arms: Argent a chevron embattled, counter-embattled, between three griffins heads erased sable, each charged with a plate.

Crest: A hind's head ppr. collared argent.

The Virginia branch descend from Sir Francis Bickley, Bart., of Attleborough Hall, Norfolk. Sir Francis, 3rd, Bart., married 2nd, Mary, daughter and co-heir of Sir Humphrey Winch, Bart. He died 1687 and is buried at St. Mary's, Attleborough. By his 1st wife he had a son, Francis, who became 4th Baronet, but d.s.p. 1746. A son, Humphrey, by the 2nd wife, became 5th Baronet and d.s.p. 1752. Joseph Bickley, brother of Humphrey, and a son of the 3rd Baronet, immigrated to Virginia, and died before 4 Dec., 1751. In 1703, this Joseph was in King and Queen county, afterwards removing to King William, and finally settling in Louisa county, of which he was the first Sheriff and Justice. He married Sarah Gessedge, widow of Richard Gessedge, and had issue, William, who succeeded as 6th Baronet on the death of his uncle, Sir Humphrey Bickley (William's father Joseph being then dead). Sir William died intestate, 3 Sept., 1771, the title going to his eldest son Joseph, who thus became the 7th Baronet. He removed in 1820 to Tennessee, and the title is now vested in the direct male heir of this line. The immigrant, Joseph Bickley, had besides his son William, 6th Bart., the following children: Joseph, Jr., John, Frances, Charles, Francis and James Bickley.

GORDON. Middlesex county.

Arms. Azure three boars heads couped or.

Wax seal on the will of William Gordon, dated 29 Feb., 1684, at Urbanna. As Lieut. William Gordon he patented 245 acres of land in Middlesex in 1672.

BLAND. James River.

Arms: Argent on a bend sable three pheons of the field.

Crest: Out of a ducal coronet or, a lion's head ppr.

Motto: Sperati et virite fortes.

The Virginia family are of the same line as Sir Thomas Bland, of Kippax Park, Yorkshire, who was created a Baronet by Charles I. 30 Aug., 1642. John Bland of Syth Lane, London, and Plaistow, Essex, born 1573, married Susan Duclere, born 1590, and had issue, seventeen children. Edwin Bland, their fifth child, married Jane, daughter of Gregory Bland, died 1653, and is buried at "Kymages," near Westover. Theodorick Bland, the fifteenth child, afterwards of "Berkeley," James River, was baptized 16 Jan., 1629, at St. Antholin's, London. He came to Virginia in 1654, and died Aug. 1669. His tombstone at Westover bears the above arms, impaling Bennett. "Or, three demi-lions rampant gules." He married Anne, daughter of Colonel Richard Bennett of Weyanoke, who was sometime Governor of Virginia. Anne Bland died Nov., 1687.

EDWARDS. Lancaster county.

Arms: Argent a fess ermines between three martlets or.

Crest: On a ducal coronet argent, a tiger passant or.

John Edwards patented 350 acres of land in Lancaster in 1653. In May, 1657, the Lancaster Court gave to him a certificate of the importation of his children, John and Mary. On 30 Nov., 1659, there is mention that he had married Frances, daughter of Francis Cole of Lancaster, decd. John Edwards's will, dated 3 Feb., 1667, proved in March of same year, bears the impression of his seal with the above arms. His will was also probated in England, in the Preg. Court of Canterbury, the 24 Nov., 1668. In it he states, "Since I left behind me in England my dear wife and three children, what I left with them, as also the produce of my Virginia estate, and the produce of the ship "Susan," to be divided into four parts to them equally."

CHURCHILL. Middlesex county.

Arms: Sable a lion rampant argent, debruised with a bendlet gules.

Crest: Out of a ducal coronet or, a demi-lion rampant argent.

William Churchill, first of the family in Virginia, was deputy sheriff of Middlesex county in 1674, and member of the Council

in 1705. According to his own deposition, he was born 1649 in
North Aston, Oxfordshire. The arms of the family on a wax seal
attached to a deed of his son Armistead, identify the family in
Virginia with the Churchills of Devon, Somerset and Dorset.
William Churchill was married twice, his first wife being Mary
————. By her, according to a deed dated 20 Dec., 1683, he had
two daughters. He married, 2nd, 5 Oct., 1703, Elizabeth, daughter
of Colonel John Armistead of Gloucester, and widow of Ralph
Wormeley, late Secretary of State. By this marriage he had: (1)
Armistead, son and heir; (2) Priscilla, born 21 Dec., 1705, mar-
ried, 1st, Robert Carter of "Nominy"; 2nd, John Lewis of Warner
Hall; (3) Elizabeth, born 1710, died 16 April, 1779, married, 1st,
Colonel William Bassett of the Council; 2nd, William Dawson,
president of William and Mary College, who died 20 July, 1752.
The will of William Churchill was dated 18 Nov., 1710; probated
10 Mch., 1710-11.

FLOWER. Lancaster county.
> Arms: Per fess argent and azure, in chief two fleurs-de-lis gules,
> in base one or.
> From wax seal on a bond of George Flower, dated 1712, at Lan-
> caster Court House.

WOODFORD. Caroline county.
> Arms: Sable, three leopards' faces or, jessant de lis.
> Crest: Two lions' gambs erased or.
> Major William Woodford, the immigrant, of "Windsor," Caroline
> county, married 2 Sept. 1732, Anne Cocke, born 1704, daughter of
> Dr. William Cocke of Williamsburg and his wife Ann Catesby,
> sister of the celebrated naturalist, Mark Catesby. They had
> issue: (1) General William Woodford, born 6 Oct., 1734, a dis-
> tinguished soldier of the French and Indian wars and afterward
> Colonel of the 2nd Va. Regiment. He was taken prisoner by the
> British and died in New York in 1780. He married Mary, daugh-
> ter of George Thornton and his wife Mildred Gregory, whose
> mother Mildred, was a sister of Augustine Washington, and Aunt
> of General George Washington. (2) Thomas, born 14 Aug., 1736,
> d.s.p. (3) Catesby, born 19 June, 1738, died 1791, married in 1771
> to Mary Buckner. (4) John, born 23 March, 1742, d.s.p. in 1763
> in London, Eng. (5) Henry, born 7 Jan., 1744, died in Caroline
> county.
> The Woodford arms are engraved on a seal of General William
> Woodford, and are also impressed in wax on several letters writ-
> ten by the General prior to 1780, some of the letters being in pos-
> session of a descendant, Dr. T. Madison Taylor of New York City.

BOLLING. Prince George county.
> Arms: Sable an inescutcheon ermine, within an orle of eight
> martlets argent.
> Robert Bolling, the first of the Virginia family, lived at Kippax,
> sometimes called Farmingdale, Prince George county. He was

born 26 Dec., 1646, and was the son of John and Mary Bolling of All Hallows, Tower Street, London, who was a descendant of the Bollings of Bolling Hall, Bradford, Yorkshire. He came to Virginia 2 Oct., 1660, and married, 1st, in 1675, Jane, daughter of Thomas Rolfe, and granddaughter of Pocahontas. He married, 2nd, in 1681, Anne, daughter of John Stith of Brunswick county. By his first wife he had issue: (1) John, born 27 Jan., 1676. By his second wife he had: (2) Robert, born 25 Jan., 1682. (3) Stith, born 28 March, 1686. (4) Edward, born 3 Oct., 1687. (5) Anne, born 22 July, 1690. (6) Drury, born 21 June, 1695. (7) Thomas, born 20 March, 1697. (8) Agnes, born 30 Nov., 1700. Robert Bolling died 17 July, 1709. An extended pedigree of the family will be found in the "Bolling Memoirs."

DUKE. Albemarle county.

Arms: Azure a chevron between three birds close argent, membered gules.

Crest: A sword argent, hilt or, stuck in a plume of five ostrich feathers, two azure, three argent.

Motto: In adversis idem.

The immigrant of this family was George Duke, who in Jan., 1656, being then a prisoner of the Parliamentarians at Exeter, petitioned to be transported to Virginia, which was granted. His son, Henry Duke, was a Justice of James City county in 1680, Burgess in 1692 and 1699, and Councillor in 1703. He married Lydia, daughter of Charles Hansford. Their son, Cliviers Duke, used the above arms on a seal ring, and they are also engraved on old silverware, now in the possession of R. T. W. Duke, Esq., of Charlottesville, a greatgrandson of Cliviers Duke. The arms are identical with those of Duke of Benhall Lodge and Brompton, Suffolk.

BOWIE. Stafford county.

Arms: Argent on a bend sable three buckles or.

Crest: A demi-lion azure, holding in the dexter paw a dagger.

Motto: Quod non pro patria

Arms taken from an old seal owned by Mr. John Bowie Gray of "Travellers' Rest," Stafford county. The seal had been the property of his grandfather John Gray, who was born in Scotland, it being in turn the seal of the latter's maternal grandfather, John Bowie of Scotland, whose daughter Isabella married William Gray, the said John Gray's father.

LAMAR.

Arms: Gules two lions passant guardant in pale or.

Crest: A mermaid ppr. holding in the sinister hand a mirror, and in the dexter a comb.

The Lamars were Huguenot refugees from Anjou, France, and came to Virginia about 1660. In the records of Annapolis, Maryland, is the following entry: "17 Nov., 1663. Whereas, Thomas and Peter Lamar or Lamore, late of Virginia, and subjects of the

Crown of France, have transported themselves into this Province, there to abide, and have besought us to grant them leave to here inhabit as full denizens, etc., etc." The coat of arms is engraved on old silver, and an ancient seal, still in possession of members of the family.

FARRAR. Henrico county.
    Arms: Argent on a bend sable three horseshoes of the field.
    Crest: A horseshoe sable, between two wings argent.
    Motto: Ferre va ferme.
    The Virginia family descend from Nicholas Farrar of London, born 1546, and whose will was probated in that city 4 April, 1620. He married Mary Wodenoth of Cheshire, who was living at the time of her husband's death. Nicholas Farrar was a member of the Virginia Company. He had issue: (1) Sussannah, married John Collett;. (2) John, born 1590, died 1657, married Bathsheba ————, and had a daughter, Virginia; he was Treasurer of the Virginia Company. (3) Nicholas, born 22 Feb., 1593; also Treasurer of the Virginia Company. (4) Richard, born 1596. (5) William, Barrister at Law, was in Virginia in 1621, died ante 1637; he was member of the Council 1627-33, Justice of Charles City and Henrico, and left issue: William, son and heir of Henrico, and John. The arms used by the above are those of Farrar of Hull, Yorkshire.

ROLFE. Jamestown.
    Arms: Gyronny of eight or and azure, on a chief sable three annulets argent.
    Crest: A lion's head erased argent, fretty gules.
    John Rolfe, gent., was born 6 May, 1585, and was the son of John Rolfe and Dorothea Mason of Heacham, Norfolk. He came to Virginia June, 1608, and was wrecked on the Bermudas, where, by his first wife, whom he married in England, he had a daughter born to him, called Bermuda. His second wife was the celebrated Pocahontas, daughter of Powhatan, by whom he had a son, Thomas, who has descendants in Virginia. His third wife was Jane, daughter of Captain William Pierce, by whom he had a daughter, Elizabeth. John Rolfe was Recorder of Virginia from 1614 to 1619. Thomas Rolfe, the son of Pocahontas, was educated in England by his uncle, Henry Rolfe. He afterward resided in Virginia and married a Miss Poythress, and had a son, Anthony of England, and a daughter, Jane, who married Robert Bolling of Virginia.

BRENT. Stafford county.
    Arms: Gules a wyvern argent.
    Crest: A wyvern's head between two wings expanded argent.
    Motto: Silentio et diligentia.
    George Brent of Woodstock, Stafford county, was the sixth son of George Brent of Cossington, Somerset, and Marianna, daughter of Sir John Peyton of Doddington, Isle of Ely. He married the

daughter of Captain William Green and niece of Sir William Layton, by whom he had issue: George, Nicholas, Robert, Marianne and Elizabeth. He married, secondly, on 27 March, 1687, the second daughter of Lady Baltimore, by her first husband, Henry Sewell. George Brent' was appointed in 1683 Receiver-General, North of the Rappahannock River. He was a nephew of Giles Brent, who was Governor and Admiral of Maryland, 1643.

PRATT. Gloucester county.

Arms: Argent on a chevron sable, between three pellets each charged with a martlet of the field, as many mascles or.

Crest: A wolf's head erased per pale argent and sable.

William Pratt, merchant of Gloucester, married 4 Sept., 1720, Elizabeth, born 29 Aug., 1701, daughter of Dr. William Cocke of Williamsburg. They had issue, three children, two of whom died young. The second daughter, Elizabeth, was married 24 Feb., 1742, to Walter King of Williamsburg. Wax impressions of the Pratt arms are found on letters written by various members of the family dating from 1724 and correspond with the arms of Pratt of the county of Norfolk.

CLOPTON. York and New Kent counties.

Arms: Sable a bend ermine between two cotises dancette or, a mullet for difference.

Crest: A wolf's head per pale or and azure.

William Clopton, born in England in 1655, was constable of York-Hampton in 1682. He was also Justice of New Kent. He married Ann, widow of Thomas Dennett, and daughter of Robert Booth, Clerk of York county. Her tomb in St. Peter's churchyard, New Kent, bears the Clopton arms. She died in 1716, aged 70 years, leaving three sons, Robert, William and Walter, and two daughters, Ann and Elizabeth. A deed of William Clopton, Jr., dated 22 July, 1710, bears a wax seal with the above arms. They are the same as those of Clopton of the county of Suffolk, Eng. In the St. Peters parish register, New Kent, are numerous entries pertaining to the family.

WALKE. Norfolk county.

Arms: Gules a chevron between three crosses croslet argent, on a chief of the last a buck's head cabossed of the first.

Crest: A buck's head erased ppr.

Motto: Fear God.

Thomas Walke, merchant, came from the Barbadoes, and was in Norfolk county in 1662. He married Mary, daughter of Colonel Anthony Lawson and had issue: Thomas, Anthony and Mary. Thomas Walke, Jr., died 1723. He married Katherine ————, and had issue: Thomas and Anthony, Elizabeth and Katherine. He was Lieut.-Colonel of Militia and was a member of the House of Burgesses in 1714. The arms of this family are registered in the office of Ulster Herald, Dublin.

HARRISON. Williamsburg.

Benjamin Harrison, Jr., one of the feofees of Williamsburg in 1700, used a shield, the charge in same consisting of a chevron. (Ludwell MSS.)

TURBERVILLE. Westmoreland county.

Arms: Ermine a lion rampant gules, ducally crowned or.

The tomb of Frances Turberville on Booth's Plantation, has the above arms upon it. She was the eldest child of Henry Ashton, and was born in 1699, died 24 April, 1720, and married 24 April, 1718, to George Turberville, gent., by whom a daughter, Elizabeth, born 12 Jan., 1719. Another tomb at the same place is that of Lettice Turberville, born 15 July, 1707, daughter of William Fitzhugh, by Ann, his wife, who was daughter of the Hon. Richard Lee. She married Capt. George Turberville 16 May, 1727, and died 10 Feb., 1732. This tomb bears the above arms, impaling Corbin, the latter being, "Ermine on a chief or three ravens sable." The first of the Turberville family in Virginia, was John, who was in Lancaster county in 1633. The arms used by the Virginia branch correspond with those of Turberville of Beere Regis, Dorset.

HUBARD. Williamsburg.

Arms: Sable an estoile of six points, in chief a crescent argent between two flaunches ermine.

Crest: A Sagittarius statant.

Motto: Fortis et fidelis.

The above arms are on a book-plate of James Hubard of the city of Williamsburg, and are pasted in a book which was printed in London in 1735. The arms are in pale, in the dexter being an unidentified coat, viz.: "Argent upon a chevron gules between three pheons sable, five mullets of the field." The Hubard quartering is somewhat similar to Hubbard of the county of Durham.

BRISTOW. Gloucester county.

Arms: Ermine on a fess cotised sable, three crescents or.

Crest: Out of a crescent or, a demi-eagle displayed azure.

Motto: Vigilantibus non dormientibus.

Robert Bristow of Ayot St. Lawrence, Herts, was born 1643, the second son of Robert Bristow, and was descended from Nicholas Bristow, Clerk of the Jewels to Henry VIII., Edward VI., Queen Mary and Queen Elizabeth. He came to Virginia in 1660, settling in Gloucester county, where he married Averilla, daughter of Major Robert Curtis and was eventually a Colonel of Militia. He returned to England in 1677 and became a merchant in London, where his will was probated 29 Nov., 1707. An extended pedigree of the English branch of the family is contained in the "Visitation of Herts, 1634," and in "Burke's Landed Gentry."

LISTER. Henrico county.

Arms: Ermine on a fesse sable, three mullets argent, a canton gules.

Crest: A stag's head erased ppr. charged on the neck with a trefoil slipped gules.

Motto: Justus propositi tenax.

Thomas Lister, fifth son of James Lister of Shipden Hall, Yorkshire, and Mary, daughter of William Issot, was born at Halifax, 9 Dec., 1708, died 15 Aug., 1740, in Virginia, and married 1733, Anne, daughter of John Lewis. They had issue: (1) William, born 7 July, 1734, married 1760 Margaret Lewis of Langhorne. They left Virginia and settled at Langhorne Caermarthen, Wales. (2) Martha, married R. Burch of Virginia. (3) Mary, died young. (4) Susanna, married R. Morris of Virginia.

William Lister, a brother of Thomas, baptized 3 Apr., 1712, also settled in Virginia, and married in 1738 Susanna Lewis and had issue, two daughters. He died 21 Oct., 1743. The Listers are descended from Richard Lister, who was Constable of Halifax, A. D. 1412 (Dugdale's Visitation of Yorks).

COCKE. Williamsburg.

Arms: Argent a fesse sable between two talbots passant.

Dr. William Cocke, an English physician, born at Sudbury, Suffolk, in 1662, educated at Queen's College, Cambridge, died at Williamsburg in 1720. He was a member of the Council, Secretary of State for Virginia and Judge of the General Court. He married Elizabeth, sister of Mark Catesby, the celebrated naturalist. The Catesby arms, used on a letter written by the naturalist, dated 22 June, 1722, are: "Argent two lions passant sable crowned or." Catesby Cocke, son of Dr. William Cocke, born 1702, resided at Belmont, Fairfax county, and on a deed made by him 4 Jan., 1724, are the Cocke arms as given above.

BROWNE. Essex county.

Arms: Ermine on a bend gules three lions rampant or.

Crest: A griffin's head.

Wax seal on the will of Buckner Browne of Essex, probated at Tappahannock 19 Aug., 1735.

CODD. Northumberland county.

Arms: Argent a fesse embattled sable between three pellets.

Col. St. Leger Codd was the son of William Codd of Pelicans, Kent, and his wife Mary, daughter of Sir Warham St. Leger of Ulcombe, Kent, whom he married in 1632. Col. Codd was one of the Commissioners to superintend the building of a fort on the Potomac in 1671. He was Justice of Northumberland county 1677, Presiding Justice 1680 and Member of the House of Burgesses 1680 and 1682. He soon afterward removed to Maryland. He was married twice, his first wife being a daughter of Richard Perrott of Lancaster county, Virginia, by whom he had two sons, James and Berkeley. His second wife was Anna Bland, the widow of Theodorick Bland and daughter of Col. Richard Bennett. By her he had a son, St. Leger, and daughters, Beatrix and Sarah. His will, dated 7 Nov., 1706, was proved in Maryland 9 Feb., 1707-8, and in Lancaster, Va., 8 Apr., 1708.

SLAUGHTER. Essex county.

Arms: Argent a saltire azure.

The above arms are on a seal to the bond of William Slaughter as Sheriff of Essex in 1685. They are similar to the arms of Slaughter of the counties of Gloucester, Hereford and Worcester, Eng. The crest for the English arms being, "Out of a ducal coronet or. an eagle's head between two wings expanded azure, beaked gold."

LATANE. Essex county.

Arms: Argent a fesse between three crescents sable.

Crest: A crane's head volant argent.

Arms on the will of the Rev. Lewis Latane, probated in Essex 17 Apr., 1733. He was a Huguenot and fled from France to England in 1685, coming to Virginia in 1700, when he became minister of South Farnham Parish, Essex. He is said to have been married twice before coming to this country. His third wife being Mary Deane. He left a son, John, and daughters, Charlotte, Phebe, Henrietta and Marian. The son, John, married Mary Allen, who had an only surviving son, William Latane, Justice of Essex 1760 to 1780 and who married Ann, sister of Col. Thomas Waring of Goldberry, Essex. He had issue: (1) Mary, married John Temple; (2) Lucy, married Payne Waring of Essex; (3) John, married and had issue; (4) Henry W., born 1777, member of the House of Delegates from Essex 1815-16, married and had issue; (5) Thomas, died 1837, married Mary, daughter of Nelson Berkeley of Hanover county; (6) William C.; (7) Ann S., married ——— Lewis; (8) Eliza, married ——— Waring.

FLOWER. Gloucester county.

Arms. Sable a unicorn passant or, on a chief argent three pinks gules, stalked and leaved vert.

On the tomb of Jeffrey Flower in Abington churchyard, Gloucester, are the above arms. The inscription states that he died 2 Sept., 1726, aged 38 years. The arms are the same as Flower of Chilton, county Wilts. He died intestate and in the Preg. C. C. Letters of Administration were granted to Noblett Rubock, attorney for Lucie Flower, now in Ireland, mother of defunct, 1 Feb., 1725-6. His administrator in Virginia was Peter Whiting.

BROWNE. King William county.

Arms: Argent on a bend double cotised sable, three spread eagles of the first.

Crest: An eagle displayed argent, on the wings two bars sa.

Herbert Claiborne, born 7 Apr., 1746, of King William Co., married, 2nd, a daughter of William Burnet Browne of Elsing Green, who settled a large estate upon his eldest grandson upon condition of his taking the name of William Burnet Browne. William

Burnet was a son of William Browne of Beverly, Mass., who married a daughter of William, the son of Bishop Gilbert Burnet, and was Provincial Governor of New York and Massachusetts. He traced descent from Sir Thomas Browne, Treasurer of the Household to Henry VI., from whom in succession Sir Anthony, Standard Bearer to Henry VII., and Sir Anthony, created Viscount Montacute.

COLE. Warwick county.

Arms: Argent and vert a cross lozengy.

Crest: Out of a coronet a dexter hand.

Col. William Cole is believed to have been a son of William Cole, who represented Nutmeg Quarter in the House of Burgesses in 1629. He was Secretary of State 17 Jan., 1690, and Member of the Council, 1674-5. He died 4th of March, 1693-4, aged 56 years, and the above arms are inscribed upon his tomb. He was thrice married, his last two wives being respectively, Anne, daughter of Gov. Edward Digges, and Martha, daughter of Col. John Lear. By the latter he had a son, William, who was a member of the House of Burgesses in 1718 and 1726, Deputy Receiver-General in 1721, and Colonel of Militia. By his first wife Col. Cole (1693) had a daughter, Susannah, who married Dudley Digges. She died 1708, aged 34 years.

LANDON. Lancaster county.

Arms: Gyronny of eight or and azure, an inescutcheon argent.

Crest: A lizard ppr.

Motto: Ma force d'en haut.

The tomb of Elizabeth Carter at Christ Church, Lancaster, states that she was the second wife of Robert Carter, and dau. of Thomas and Mary Landon of Grednal, Herefordshire. She bore her husband ten children and died 3 July, 1719, in the 36th year of her age and 19th of her marriage.

Thomas Landon, the father of Elizabeth Carter, was the son of Silvanus Landon, who was probably the son of John Landon, Yeoman of the Wine Cellar to James I. and Charles I. The will of Thomas Landon is at Middlesex Court House, dated 9 Nov., 1700, probated 3 Feb., 1700-1. He had issue: William, Thomas, Roger, Silvanus, John, Mary, Ann, St. Leger, Elizabeth. Mary, the daughter of the first Thomas Landon, married, 1st, John Jones, and, 2nd, Alexander Swan, whose will, dated 14 March, 1709, was probated in Lancaster Co., Va., 10 May, 1710.

SPENCER. Westmoreland county.

Arms: Quarterly. 1st and 4th, or and gules; 2nd and 3rd, a fret of the first, on a bend sable three fleurs de lis argent.

Crest: Out of a ducal coronet gules, a griffin's head argent collared or, between two wings expanded of the third, charged on the head and on each wing a fleur de lis sable, and on the neck a crescent.

Nicholas Spencer, Secretary of Virginia and Acting Governor

Sept., 1683, was the second son of Nicholas Spencer, Esq., of Cople, Bedfordshire, by Mary, daughter of Sir Edward Castwick of Wellington, Beds. He died 23 Sept., 1689. His wife was Frances, daughter of Col. John Mottrom of Northumberland county, by whom he had several children. For English pedigree of the family, see "Visitation of Bedfordshire."

WESTWOOD. Elizabeth City and York county.

Arms: Sable a lion rampant argent crowned with a mural crown, three crosses crosslet fitchee or.

Crest: A stork's head ppr. erased and gorged with a mural crown or.

The above emblazoning is in possession of W. J. Westwood, Esq., of Richmond, to whom it descended from his grandfather.

JENINGS. Gloucester and York counties.

Arms: Argent a chevron between three plummets sable.

Crest: A griffin's head couped behind two wings inverted ppr. in the beak a plummet pendent sable.

Edmund Jenings, son of Sir Edmund Jenings of Ripon and Margaret, daughter of Sir Edward Barkham, Lord Mayor of London 1621, was clerk of York County, Attorney-General, Secretary of state and President of the Council. He was born in 1659, and died 2 June, 1727. He married Frances, daughter of Henry Corbin, and had issue: Frances, who married Charles Grymes of Moratico, Richmond Co.; Elizabeth, who married Richard Porteus of Gloucester Co., and Edmund of Maryland.

Col. Peter Jenings of Gloucester Co. was probably a brother of Edmund Jenings, as the latter had a brother named Peter (see "La Neves' Knights"). He was Attorney-General for Virginia and died 1671. He married Catharine, daughter of Sir Thomas Lunsford. She died 17 May, 1685, having married, 2nd, Ralph Wormley. The Peter Jenings of Gloucester Co., mentioned in the Abington Parish Register, was probably a son of the first Peter. The following entries are found in the Register: "Children of Peter and Sarah Jenings, Philip, baptized — Apr., 1678; Elizabeth, born 23 Feb., 1684; Thomas, baptized 20 Feb., 1686; Rebecca, baptized 18 May, 1690.

JONES. Sussex county.

Arms: Ermine three lions.

From the book plate of Robert Jones, King's Attorney for North Carolina, 1761-67. He was the son of Robert Jones of Sussex county, Va.

CALTHORPE. York county.

Arms: Chequy, or and azure, a fesse ermine.

Crest: A salamander or. in flames ppr.

Col. Christopher Calthorpe was in Virginia as early as 1623. In 1635 he obtained two patents of land in Elizabeth City county. He was a Justice of York county in 1658, and Member of the

House of Burgesses in 1659. On 24 Apr., 1662, Anne Calthorpe, the relict of Christopher Calthorpe, petitioned the court for letters of administration on the estate of her deceased husband. She died 9 Dec., 1667. On 21 Jan., 1667, the children of Christopher Calthorpe petitioned for a division of the estate, and on the 11th of Dec., 1671, the Justices of York county gave a release to the administrator of the estate, the following children being named: James, Barbara and Ann. From the Parish Register we find that Barbara was buried 28 July, 1680, and Ann buried 7 Apr., 1685. James, the son, was a Justice of York county. He died 3 Aug., 1689, married Anne ————, who died 24 Aug., 1698, and had issue, six children.

Col. Christopher Calthorpe was the second son of Christopher Calthorpe by his wife Maude, daughter and co-heir of John Thurton of Brome, Norfolk. An extended pedigree of the English family is found in "Le Neve's Knights" and "Blomefield's History of Norfolk."

LYDDALL. New Kent county.

Arms: Argent, fretty gules on a chief of the last three leopards' faces or.

Col. George Lyddall of the above county was a son of Sir Thomas Lyddall of Ravenholm Castle, Durham, and his wife, Bridget, daughter of Edward Woodward of Lee. She was Maid of Honor to the Queen of Bohemia. She married, 2nd, Thomas Heneage of Greys Inn, Surrey (Le Neve's Knights). Col. George Lyddall died 19 Jan., 1705 (St. Peter's Parish Register, New Kent).

THOMPSON. Elizabeth City.

Arms: Or on a fesse dancette azure, three estoiles argent on a canton of the second the sun in glory ppr.

Crest: An arm erect, vested gules, cuffed argent, holding in the hand ppr. five ears of wheat or.

Motto: In Lumine Lucem.

Ralph Thompson of Walton, Herts, married Elizabeth, daughter of John Harsnett (Visitation of Herts, 1634). They had issue: (1) Maurice, who was in Virginia in 1620, returned to England and his eldest son, Sir John, became first Baron Haversham in 1696; (2) Col. George Thompson, born 1603, was member of the House of Burgesses for Elizabeth City in 1629; (3) Sir William Thompson, born 1614, came to Virginia but returned to England, and became Governor of the East Indies temp. Charles II.; (4) Paul Thompson, born 1611, was in Virginia in 1623; (5) Major Robert Thompson was in New England; (6) Elizabeth; (7) Mary, born 1599, married Capt. William Tucker, born 1589, who was in Virginia 1610, member of the House of Burgesses 1623, member of the Council 1626, and had issue: Elizabeth, born in Virginia in 1624-5.

WHITEHEAD. King William county.

Arms: Azure on a chevron between three buglehorns or, three

martlets of the field.

Crest: Out of a celestial crown or, a buglehorn between two wings.

The above arms are on a wax seal of a deed of Richard Whitehead of Gloucester county to William Beck of New Kent for 5,000 acres of land granted to said Whitehead 24 Oct., 1673. The deed is dated 5 June, 1699. There is also another wax impression on a deed of Philip Whitehead of King William county, gent., and Elizabeth, his wife, to Edmund Berkeley of Gloucester county, for 2,000 acres in King William county, being part of a patent of 5,000 acres granted to Mr. Richard Whitehead 26 Oct., 1699, part of which was given to said Philip by deed of gift from said Richard and part by will of said Richard, dated 13 May, 1701. This deed is recorded 20 Nov., 1707, and upon it, beside the Whitehead arms, is another wax impression opposite the name of Elizabeth Whitehead, which seems to be "a saltire with four nags' heads." The above original deeds, together with others, are in the possession of Major William Noland Berkeley of Charlottesville. From them we find that Richard Whitehead lived in Gloucester county in 1699 and had two children: Philip of King William, and Mary, an elder daughter, who, before 1698, was married to Philip Ryan of King and Queen county and had a son Whitehead Ryan. The arms on the seal are those of Whitehead, Lancashire, Eng.

STRACHEY. York county.

Arms: Argent a cross between four eaglets gules.

Crest: An eagle displayed gules, charged upon the breast with a cross crosslet fitchee argent.

William Strachey, Recorder of Virginia, was at Jamestown in 1610. He was descended from the Stracheys of Saffron Walden, Essex, and Sutton Court, Somerset. William Strachey married Frances Foster and they had: William, who died in 1634 and who married, 1st, Eleanor Read, by whom a son, William, who came to Virginia in 1686. This William left a daughter, Arabella, who married Henry Cox of Essex county. William Strachey (1634) married, 2nd, Elizabeth Cross, niece of Sir Robert Cross, by whom he had John Strachey (1634-1674), whose grandson, Dr. John Strachey, came to Virginia and has now descendants by the name of Mastin living in Alabama.

HARWARD. Lancaster county.

Arms: A cross fleury.

Crest: A stag's head.

From a wax seal on the will of George Harward, dated 5 Jan., 1703, at Lancaster Court House. The tinctures cannot be distinguished, and there is no English family of the name bearing similar arms. The Harwoods of Berks and Salop have for a crest "A stag's head cabossed."

JAQUELIN. Or three nags' heads gules.

Crest: A nag's head.

Motto: Comme je trouve.

Edward Jaquelin, the immigrant, was a son of John Jaquelin and Elizabeth Craddock, and came to Virginia in 1697. He was born in 1668 and died 1730. He was twice married, his second wife being Martha, daughter of William Cary of Warwick county, and granddaughter of Col. Miles Cary, who came to Virginia in 1645. An oil painting of the immigrant, bearing the above arms upon its frame, is in possession of his descendants.

INGLIS. Williamsburg.

Arms: Gules on a bend, three eagles displayed, between two (unidentified) charges. (Ludwell MS.)

A wax seal of arms is on a deed dated 1700, of Mungo Inglis. He was the first Grammar Master of William and Mary College, and one of the feofees of Williamburg.

GOODWIN. York county.

At Back Creek is the tomb of Rachel, born 1630, died 23 May, 1666, the first wife of Major James Goodwin. The arms engraven upon it are almost obliterated. The shield is impaled; the dexter is much defaced, but in the chief there is a lozenge. In the sinister, which is divided quarterly, there is, 1st and 4th, a bend; 2nd and 3rd, three bars. It is possible that Rachel was a sister of John Porter, for whom Major James Goodwin obtained "head rights," the arms of Porter, Warwick, Eng., being "sable, three bars argent." In the Goodwin genealogy, compiled by Judge John S. Goodwin, the theory is advanced that Maj. James was a son of Peter Goodwin of London (Visitation of London, 1633). The arms of Peter Goodwin of London do not contain the lozenge and the latter is traceable on the dexter side of the arms of Rachel Goodwin. It may be that the arms on the dexter side are those of Goodwin of London, exemplified in 1640, viz.: "or a lion passant, guardant sable on a chief gules three lozenges vair." These are the only Goodwin arms containing a lozenge. The dexter side of the shield on the tomb being much worn, it is possible that the two other lozenges have been obliterated. The arms of Peter Goodwin of London are: "Per pale or and gules, a lion rampant between three fleur de lis counterchanged."

JERDONE. Louisa county.

Arms: Argent, a saltire and chief gules, the last charged with three mullets of the field.

Crest: A spur-rowel-of six points argent.

Motto: Cave adsum.

Francis Jerdone of Louisa county, was born at Jedburgh, Scot., 30 Jan., 1720-1, married Sarah Macon of New Kent county, Va., 10 Feb., 1753. He was the son of John Jerdone, born 7 July, 1680, a Magistrate of Jedburgh, who was the son of Adam Jerdone. The immigrant brought over with him some old silver, on which is engraved the above arms, the same being in the possession of his descendants at Shirley, Charles City county. The crest and motto is identical with that of Jardine of Applegirth, county Dum-fries, Bart., 1672, and it is evident that the immigrant was a cadet of that family.

COOKE. Gloucester county.

Arms: Or, a fesse between two lions passant gules.

Crest: A wolf's head argent, ducally gorged gules.

Arms on the tomb of Mary Booth, died 21 Jan., 1723, wife of Thomas Booth and daughter of Mordecai Cooke at Jarvis' Farm, Ware River, Gloucester. The above arms are impaled with Booth: "Argent three boars' heads erect sable," which are the arms of Booth of Barton, county Lancaster. The Cooke arms are the same as Cooke of Whitefield, county Suffolk. The first of the Cooke family in Virginia was Mordecai of Gloucester county, 1650. His wife's name is unknown, but he had issue: Mordecai, Thomas, Giles, John, Mary, Francis, Susannah and possibly others.

DANDRIDGE. King William county.

Arms: Azure, a lion's head erased or, between three mascles argent.

Crest: A lion's head erased, charged with a mascle argent.

Col. William Dandridge of Elsing Green, King William county, married, 1st, Euphan, daughter of the Rev. James Wallace, and widow of William Roscow of Warwick county. Her tomb bears the arms of Wallace impaling Dandridge. Colonel Dandridge, who died in 1743, married, 2nd, 17 March, 1719, Unity, only child of Col. Nathaniel West. Col. John Dandridge of New Kent county, brother of Col. William, married Frances, daughter of Orlando Jones, and had issue: Martha, born 2 June, 1731; John, born 23 Feb., 1732, died 23 July, 1749; William, born 2 March, 1734, died 22 Jan., 1776; Bartholomew, born 25 Dec., 1737, died 18 April, 1785; Anna Maria, born 30 March, 1739, died 17 Dec., 1777; Frances, born 2 Nov., 1744; Mary, born 4 April, 1756, died 25 Sept., 1763.

Col. John Dandridge died 31 August, 1756, aged 56 years, and is buried in St. George's churchyard, Fredericksburg. His wife died 9 April, 1785, in her 75th year.

Martha, the eldest child, born 1731, died 22 May, 1802, married 1749, Col. Daniel Parke Custis, who died 1757. She married, 2nd, 6 Jan., 1759, Col. George Washington.

The arms of the Virginia family are the same as Dandridge of Great Malvern, Worcestershire.

HALL. Prince George county.

Arms: Three tigers' heads.

Crest: A lion rampant.

In the "Virginia Gazette" of 7 Jan., 1739, is an advertisement, "Lost, some time in August last, a silver snuff box, gilt on the inside and a coat of arms being engraved on the lid, three tygers heads, and the Crest a Lyon Rampant. Whosoever brings it to Mr. Thomas Hall in Prince George county, or to the printer of this paper shall have a Pistole Reward."

The advertiser was Thomas Hall, who married Molly, daughter of Major Henry Power of James city, in 1737, and granddaughter of Dr. Henry Power and Mary, his wife, daughter of the Rev. Edward Folliott of Hampton Parish. Thomas Hall is believed to have been a grandson of Thomas Hall, Clerk of New Kent county, who was executed in 1676, as a supporter of Bacon.

NELSON. York county.

Arms: Per pale argent and sable a chevron between three fleurs de lis counterchanged.

Crest: A fleur de lis as in the arms.

Thomas Nelson, born 20 Feb., 1677, at Penrith, Cumberland, Eng., was a son of Hugh and Sarah Nelson, and died at Yorktown, 7 Oct., 1745. He married, 1st, Margaret, daughter of Robert Reade, the eldest son of Col. George Reade, Secretary of the Colony. His 2nd wife was Frances Tucker, widow of Robert Tucker of Barbadoes. The above arms are engraved on the tomb of Thomas Nelson at Yorktown. Thomas Nelson, a son by the first wife, was born in 1716, died 1784, married Lucy, daughter of Henry and Martha (Burwell) Armistead. He was Secretary of State in 1744, and remained in that office until the Revolution. Another son was William Nelson, member of the Council and acting Governor. Thomas, son of William Nelson, was a Signer of the Declaration of Independence, Governor of Virginia, and Commander of the State Militia at Yorktown.

RICHARDS. Gloucester county.

Arms: Sable a chevron between three fleur de lis or.

Arms on the tomb of the Rev. John Richards in the chancel of Ware Church, Gloucester. The inscription states that he was late rector of Nettlestead and vicar of Teston, in the county of Kent, Kingdom of England, and minister of Ware, Colony of Va. He died 12 Nov., 1735, aged 46 years. The tomb of his wife, lying near, states that she died 21 Nov., 1725, aged 40 years.

WITHAM.

Arms: Quarterly, 1st and 4th. Or three ravens sable, over all a bendlet gules, a crescent for difference. 2nd Gules a chief argent. 3rd Argent on a fesse gules between three popinjays vert, collared and membered of the second, as many escallops of the field. In Dugdale's Visitation of Yorkshire, taken in 1665, there is a Cuthbert Witham as "a merchant in Virginia." He was a son of William Witham, born 13 April, 1591, and Anne, daughter of John Flower of Methley. Cuthbert married Lucy, dau. of Francis Lascelles.

FILMER. Warwick county.

Arms: Barry of six, or and sable, on a chief of the last three cinquefoils of the first.

Crest: A falcon volant ppr. beaked and legged or, standing on a ruined castle of the last.

Henry Filmer, Member of the House of Burgesses for James City county 1642, Justice of Warwick 1647, had land grants as early as 1637 in James City county. He was a son of Sir Robert Filmer, Knt., of East Sutton, Kent, who married Anne, daughter of Martin Heton, Lord Bishop of Ely.

In the Isle of Wight Records is a Bill of Exchange, dated 16 June, 1668, "on Mr. Robert Filmer, Esq., of London," and signed "Your loving uncle, Henry Filmer." The above Robert was created a Baronet in 1675.

DIGGES. York county.

Arms: Gules on a cross argent, five double-headed eagles' heads erased sable; a crescent for difference.

Edward Digges, son of Sir Dudley Digges of Chilham, Kent, Master of the Rolls, was born 1621, and died 15 March, 1675-6. He entered Greys' Inn 19 May, 1637, and came to Virginia in 1650, settling at "Belfield," on York River. He was a member of the Council in 1654, Auditor-General 1670-75, and Governor from 31 March, 1655, to 13 March, 1657. His wife Elizabeth, who died about 1691, is believed to have been a sister of Col. John Page of York county. By her he had six sons and seven daughters. The Digges arms are on the tomb of Dudley Digges at Belfield.

PRENTIS. Suffolk county.

Arms: Per chevron or and sable, three greyhounds courant and counterchanged, collared gules.

Crest: A demi greyhound rampant or, collared, ringed and lined sable. The line coiled in a knot at the end.

The above emblazoning is in possession of the Prentis family, and has been handed down from Joseph Prentis, who was Judge of the Admiralty Court in 1776, Speaker of the House of Delegates in 1787, and Judge of the General Court of Virginia. He was a son of William Prentis of York county, whose will was probated 19 Aug., 1765, in which he mentions his sons John, Joseph, Daniel and William, and daughters Sarah, wife of William Waters, and Elizabeth Prentis. The arms are the same as those of Prentys of Wygenhall and Burston, Norfolk.

CLAYTON. Gloucester county.

Arms: Argent a cross engrailed sable, between four pellets.

Crest: A leopard's gamb erased and erect argent grasping a pellet.

John Clayton, born 1665, died 18 Nov., 1737, appointed in 1705 Attorney-General of Virginia, Judge of the Admiralty Court, member of the House of Burgesses, and Recorder of Williamsburg. His descent is as follows: (1) Thomas Clayton, of Clayton Hall, Lancashire; (2) William Clayton, of the Inner Temple, died 1627; (3) Sir Jasper Clayton of London, Alderman, fourth son of above William; (4) Sir John Clayton of the Inner Temple and of Parsons Green, Middlesex, third son and heir, knighted 17 Nov., 1664, married Alice, daughter of Sir William Bowyer, Bart., of Denham,

Bucks, by whom he had: John of Virginia and others. The arms of Sir John Clayton, as recorded by Le Neve, differ from those used by John of Virginia, the English arms being, "Argent a cross engrailed sable, between three torteaux. Crest: A dexter arm ppr. holding a dagger, the point downward." John Clayton, the emigrant, had issue: (1) John, the eminent botanist; (2) Arthur; (3) Dr. Thomas Clayton, educated at Cambridge, married 1725 Isabella Lewis of Warner Hall, and died Oct. 12, 1739, and upon his tomb in Gloucester county we find the above arms, which are those of Clayton of the county of Lancashire.

BURWELL. Gloucester county.

Arms: Paly of six, argent and sable on a bend or a teal's head erased azure.

Crest: A lion's gamb erect and erased or, grasping three burr leaves vert.

The immigrant, Lewis Burwell, was born 5 March, 1621, died 19 Nov., 1653. He was the son of Edward Burwell and Dorothy Bedell of Bedfordshire. He married Lucy, only daughter of Capt. Robert Higginson and granddaughter of Thomas Higginson of London. He had issue: Lewis Burwell, member of the Council in 1702, died 19 Dec., 1710, who married, 1st, Abigail, daughter of Anthony Smith of Colchester, Eng. She died 12 Nov., 1693. His second wife was Martha, daughter of Col. John Lear, of Nansemond county, and widow of Col. William Cole. By his first wife he had known issue four sons and six daughters and by his second wife two sons and three daughters. Upon the tomb of the first Lewis Burwell at Carter's Creek, are the above arms.

JAMESON. Essex county.

Arms: Azure, a saltire or cantoned with four ships under sail argent.

The will of James Jameson was probated in Essex 17 Nov., 1736. In it he mentions three sons: James, Thomas and David. James, the son, born 1720, died 1766, married Mary Gaines, daughter of Daniel and Elizabeth Gaines of Essex. David, the fourth child of James and Mary Jameson, was born 15 Oct., 1757. He married Mildred, daughter of Edmund and Agnes Smith, and upon Mildred Jameson's tomb, at Temple Farm, are the above arms impaling Smith. For the latter, "Azure a chevron between three acorns slipped and leaved or." Edmund Smith was descended from the Martians and Reades of Yorktown, and through them was a kinsman of George Washington. Mildred Smith Jameson died 11 Dec., 1778, aged 46 years. David, her husband, was member of the Privy Council in 1777, Lieut.-Governor in 1781, and member of the State Senate in 1783. His will was proved at Yorktown 22 July, 1793.

CHEW. James City.

Arms: Gules, a chevron argent upon a chief azure three leopards' faces or.

John Chew came to Virginia in 1622 in the "Charitie," his wife Sarah following him in the "Seafloure" the next year. He was a Burgess in 1623, 1624-9; Colonel of Militia, and a Burgess for York county 1642-4, and Justice 1634-52. In 1651, in view of his intended marriage to Mrs. Rachel Constable, he makes a deed of certain land. In 1668 he appears to be deceased. He had at least two sons, Samuel and Joseph. Samuel removed to Maryland, and in 1659 was a member of the House of Burgesses. He married about 1658 Anne, daughter of William Ayres of Nansemond county, Va., and died 15 March, 1676-7, leaving issue, nine children. His eldest son, Samuel, had, in addition to other children, also a son Samuel, and it is from a seal belonging to the latter that the above arms are taken. They are the same, with some difference in the tinctures, as those of John Chewe, Gent., died 1639, of Bewdley, Worcestershire.

KEMPE. Lancaster county.

Arms: Gules, three garbs and a bordure engrailed or.

Crest: On a garb or, a pelican vulning herself ppr.

Motto: Lucem spero.

Richard Kempe, the immigrant, was a son of Sir Robert Kempe of Gissing, Norfolk. He was Secretary of State for Virginia in 1637. He died in 1649, and his widow, Elizabeth, married Sir Thomas Lunsford and after his death, Major-General Robert Smith. Richard Kempe left no issue, but many of the name descend from his nephew, Edmund Kempe of Lancaster county, 1655.

RICE. Rappahannock county.

Arms: Quarterly, 1st and 4th, per pale indented argent and gules; 2nd and 3rd, azure a lion rampant or.

From seals on two deeds of John Rice and Rebecca, his wife, 20 Dec., 1687.

The arms are the same as Rice of County Kerry, Ireland, the family possessing land in County Cork, temp. Edward III. and descended from Sir John Rice of Buttevant. This is one of the earliest instances of the arms of an Irish family in Virginia.

GOOCH. York county.

Arms: Paly of eight, argent and sable, a chevron of the first between three greyhounds of the second, spotted of the field.

Crest: A greyhound passant argent, spotted and collared sable.

The above arms are on the tomb of Major William Gooch, at Temple Farm, York county. They are those of Gooch of Norfolk. William Gooch represented York county in the House of Burgesses in 1654, and 31st of March, 1655, he was one of the Counsellors. He died 29 Oct., 1655, leaving a daughter Anne, who married Capt. Thomas Beale, and probably a son, William. In the York records we find that Henry Gooch was Supervisor of the estate of Major William Gooch. Henry was a Justice and Lieut.-Col. of York, and about 1661 married Millicent, widow of Robert Kinsey.

SWAN. Isle of Wight county.

Arms: Azure, a chevron ermine between three swans argent.
Crest: A demi talbot salient gules, collared or.
Arms on the tomb of Col. Thomas Swan at Swan's Point, Isle of Wight county, who died 16 Sept., 1680. His son Samuel married Sarah, daughter of William Drummond, one of the leaders in Bacon's Rebellion. The Swan family were originally of Denton Court, County of Kent.

GORDON: Lancaster county.

Arms: Azure, a pheon between three boars' heads erased or.
Crest: A stag's head ppr. attired or.
Motto: Dum vigilo tutus.
Col. James Gordon, with his brother John, came from Newry, County Down, Ireland, and settled in Lancaster county in 1738. Col. James married, 1st, Millicent, daughter of Col. Edwin Conway, of Lancaster county; married, 2nd, Mary, youngest daughter of Col. Nathaniel Harrison and his wife, Mary Cary of Surry. By the second marriage he had a daughter, Mary, born 17 July, 1752, who married the Rev. James Waddell. Col. Gordon died 2nd Jan., 1768, aged 54 years. The two brothers left many descendants in Virginia. The arms are taken from a silver tankard, formerly the property of Col. James Gordon, which is now in possession of Dr. A. A. E. Taylor of Columbus, Ohio.
The Virginia immigrants were the two oldest of the four sons of James Gordon, Esq., of Newry, Co. Down. This James being the second son of James Gordon of "Sheepbridge," Co. Down, gent. The arms they use are those of Gordon of Huntly.

THROCKMORTON. Gloucester county.

Arms: Quarterly, (1) Gules, a chevron argent three bars gemelles sable, a crescent for difference (Throckmorton); (2) Or, a fesse crenellee sable (Abberbury); (3) Argent, on a fesse crenellee between six crosses crosslet fitchee gules, three crescents of the field (Olney); (4) Sable, a chevron argent between three crescents or (De La Spine); (5) Argent, on a fesse crenellee between six crosses crosslet, patee fitchee gules, three plates (Olney); (6) Gules, three bird bolts argent (Bosam); (7) Gules, a fesse or between six gouttes d'or (Wyke); (8) Throckmorton as before.
Crest: A falcon rising belled or, charged on the breast with a crescent for difference.
The above certificate of arms was granted to John Throckmorton of Ware Parish, Va., by Ralph Bigland, Somerset Herald, 3 March, 1769.
Gabriel Throckmorton, the immigrant, of Ware Parish, was a son of John Throckmorton of Ellington, County Huntingdon. He was born 1665, died Jan., 1737, married 1690 Frances, daughter of Mordecai Cooke of Gloucester county, and left issue.

GRAHAM. Prince William county.

Arms: Quarterly, 1st and 4th, on a chief sable three escallops of the field (Graham); 2nd and 3rd, argent, three roses gules (Montrose).

Crest: A falcon ppr. beaked and armed or, killing a stork argent, armed gules.

John Graham of Prince William county was a son of John Graham who married Elizabeth, daughter of Catesby Cocke of Fairfax county, and granddaughter of Dr. William Cocke of Williamsburg. John Graham (1) was a son of John Graham of Mackinston, County Perth, whose mother, Margaret, was the eldest daughter of John Graham, descended from the Dukes of Montrose.

HILL. King and Queen county.

Arms: Azure, on a chevron between three owls argent, three mullets sable, a bordure ermine.

From a seal once the property of Col. Humphrey Hill of Hillsborough, King and Queen county. The arms are the same as Hill of Alverton, Gloucestershire. Col. Hill died in 1775, and his will was probated 13 March of that year. In it he mentions his wife, Frances, his four daughters, Mary, Frances, Ann and Elizabeth, and sons John, Humphrey, Robert, Edward, William and Baylor Hill.

KINGSMILL. James City county.

Arms: Argent, semee of crosses crosslet fitchee sable, a chevron ermine between three fers de moline of the second, a chief of the third.

In 1624, Richard Kingsmill, his wife, Jane, his son Nathaniel, aged five years, and his daughter Susan, one year old, lived near James City. Elizabeth Kingsmill, a daughter of Richard, was born 1625. She married, 1st, Col. William Tayloe, and her tomb bears the Kingsmill arms impaling Tayloe, the latter being, "Vert, a sword erect or between two lions rampant endorsed ermine." The Kingsmill arms are those of Kingsmill, County Hants, and in Berry's Genealogies we find Sir William Kingsmill married Ann Wilks of Hodwell, County Warwick, and had issue: Thomas, Richard (living in 1634 and doubtless the immigrant), Robert, Frederick, Francis and John.

LIGHTFOOT. Charles City county.

Arms: Barry of six or and gules on a bend sable, three escallops argent.

Arms on the tomb of Philip Lightfoot at Sandy Point, Charles City county. He married Alice, daughter of Henry Corbin, and the latter's arms are also impaled, namely: "Argent, on a chief or three ravens ppr.'" Philip Lightfoot was a son of John Lightfoot, Barrister, of Northamptonshire, Eng. He, with his brother John, was in Gloucester county in 1670. John married, 1st, Ann, daughter of Thomas Goodrich. He died 28 May, 1707. By his first wife he had: Alice, born 25 Dec., 1698. His second wife was Mary ———, and by her he had: Goodrich, Sherwood, Thomas and Alice. Goodrich Lightfoot married Susannah ———, and by her had: Anne, born 22 Oct., 1708; John, born 17 Feb., 1711, Goodrich, bapt. 14 Feb., 1713; Mary, born 2 Oct., 1717; William, born ———; Elizabeth, born ———.

WALLER. Spotsylvania county.

Arms: Sable, three walnut leaves or, between two bendlets argent.

Col. John Waller of Newport, Spots. Co., son of John Waller, was Sheriff of King and Queen county 1702, Justice of King William county 1705, and member of the House of Burgesses 1719. He became first Clerk of Spotsylvania in 1722. His will was proved there 1 Oct., 1754. He married Dorothy King and had: (1) Mary, married Zachary Lewis; (2) Edmund, second Clerk of Spotsylvania Co.; (3) John, third Clerk of Spotsylvania Co., who married Agnes, daughter of Capt. Thomas Carr; (4) William, born 1715; (5) Thomas; (6) Benjamin of Williamsburg. The Virginia Wallers came from Newport Pagnall, County Bucks, and in the parish register there we find the following entries: "Children of Dr. John Waller and Mary, his wife: (1) William, born 24 Sept., 1671; (2) John, born 23 Feb., 1673; (3) Mary, born 23 May, 1674; (4) Thomas, born 17 Oct., 1675; (5) Steven, born 24 Nov., 1676; (6) Benjamin, born 18 March, 1678; (7) Edmund, born 3 Feb., 1680; (8) James, born 25 May, 1683; (9) Jemima, born 31 Aug., 1684."

John Waller of Newport Pagnall, born 1673, is believed to have been the Col. John Waller of Virginia who married Dorothy King. Col. Waller's residence in Spotsylvania county was called "Newport," and the arms he used were the same as the Waller's of Bucks, of which family was the celebrated poet, Edmund Waller of Beaconsfield.

CURLE. Elizabeth City.

Arms: Vert, on a chevron or, between three fleurs de lis a cinquefoil gules.

Crest: On a mount vert, a hedgehog or.

Arms on the tomb of Thomas Curle, Gent., Justice of Elizabeth City, buried at Pembroke Farm, near Hampton. He was born 24 Nov., 1640, in the Parish of St. Michael, Lewes, Sussex, Eng., and died 30 May, 1700. He left no issue, bequeathing his property to his nephews, Pasco and Joshua, sons of his brother Pasco Curle, Justice 1688 and feofee of Hampton 1691. Another brother, Samuel Curle, was also in Virginia. The arms on the tomb are those of Curle or Kyrle, of London.

NEWCE. Elizabeth City.

Arms: Sable, two pallets argent, a canton ermine.

Sir William Newce came to Virginia with Francis Wyatt in 1621, dying the same year. His brother, Capt. Thomas Newce, came over in the winter of 1621, and was made a member of the Council. He died 1st Apr., 1623, leaving a widow and child in Virginia.

LITTLETON. Accomac county.

Arms: Argent, a chevron between three escallops sable.

Crest: A stag's head cabossed sable, attired or, between the attires a buglehorn or, hanging by a bend gules.

Col. Nathaniel Littleton was in Virginia in 1635. He was Chief Magistrate of Northampton county, and Counsellor in 1640, and Burgess in 1652. He died in 1654. He married Ann, the widow of Charles Harmar, of Accomac, and daughter of Henry Southey. Col. Littleton had issue: (1) Edward, (2) Southey, (3) Esther, (4) Mary, (?) who married Col. Edmund Scarburgh. The connection of the Virginia Littletons with Sir Edward Littleton, Lord Chief Justice of England, is shown in the pedigree book of the family in the possession of the present Lord Hatherton. The pedigree, in condensed form, as follows: 1. Sir Thomas Littleton, died 23 Aug., 1481; 2. Thomas, married Anne Batreaux; 3. John, married Alice Thomes; 4. Sir Edward of Henley, Shropshire, married Mary Walter, and they had issue: (1) Sir Edward, Lord Chief Justice; (2) William; (3) James; (4) William; (5) John; (6) Nathaniel, who came to Virginia in 1635, and who was a gentleman of the Earl of Southampton's Company in the Low Countries in 1625; (7) Timothy; (8) Anne; (9) Mary; (10) Martha; (11) Priscilla; (12) Joanne.

Col. Southey Littleton, the son of Col. Nathaniel, married, 1st, Sarah ————; 2nd, Elizabeth, daughter of Major Edmund Bowman. Gertrude, daughter of Edmund Bowman (alive 1681), married John Cropper, and the estate of Major Bowman, called "Bowman's Folly," has descended in a direct line for eight generations in the Cropper family.

DOUGLAS. Loudoun · county.

Arms: Argent, a heart imperially crowned ppr. between two buckles azure, all within a bordure gules; on a chief of the third three stars of the field.

Crest: A heart ppr.

Motto: Fortis et fidelis.

Col. William Douglas of Loudoun county, was a son of Hugh Douglas, Esq., of Garallan, Ayrshire, a descendant of Douglas, Earl of Drumlanrig, and the Earls of Douglas. Col. Douglas was a Justice in 1770, and High Sheriff in 1780. His will was probated in March Court 1783.

LONG. New Kent county.

Arms: A lion rampant.

Crest: A lion's head.

From arms on a tomb at Blissland, New Kent, of Mr. John Long of Ramsgate, in the county of Kent, in Great Britain, Commander of the ship "John and Mary," who departed this life 24 July, 1736, aged 25 years.

PLACE.

Arms: Per pale or and gules, a lion passant guardant counterchanged.

Crest: Out of a ducal coronet or, a dexter arm embowed in armor, holding in the hand a battle axe all ppr.

Rowland Place, of Dinsdale, county Durham, born 1642, died 1713, married Priscilla, daughter of Sir John Brooks of Norton, Yorkshire, Bart. He was a member of the Virginia Council in 1680. (Familiae Minorum Gentium, p3. 921.)

DOODES. Middlesex county.

On the will of Minor Doodes at Urbanna, Middlesex, dated 13 Dec., 1677, is a seal, bearing the impression of a 17th Century ship with three masts and resting on water. The same seal is also impressed on the will of his wife, Mary Doodes. Among the Dutch immigrants who came to Virginia about 1650, was a merchant who signed himself indifferently Doodes Minor and Minor or Mindert Doodes. As Minor Doodes of Nansemond county, he signs a deed in 1655, and in 1665 he and his wife Mary, hailing from Lancaster county, unite in a deed to Peter Montague. The will of Mary Doodes mentions a daughter, Marie Montague, and her daughter Marie; sons Doodes Mindert and Peter Montague. The will of the last named Doodes Minor, dated 13 Nov., 1694, mentions his wife Elizabeth and four sons: Minor, William, Garrett and Peter. In the Christ Church Parish Register, Middlesex, are a number of entries pertaining to this family.

HERBERT. Dinwiddie county.

Arms: Per pale, azure and gules, three lions rampant argent, armed and langued or.

Crest: A bundle of arrows or, headed and feathered argent, six in saltire, one in pale; girt round the middle with a belt gules, buckle and point extended of the first.

The above arms are engraved on the tomb of John Herbert of Prince George county, which was taken from the family residence "Puddledock," in Dinwiddie county (formerly part of Prince George) to Blandford churchyard at Petersburg. According to the inscription on the tomb, he died 17 March, 1704, aged 46 years, and was the son of John Herbert, apothecary of London, and grandson of Richard Herbert, citizen and grocer of London. He married Frances, sister of John Anderson, of Prince George county, she marrying secondly, Peter Wynne. Her will was proved in 1726-7. By her first husband she had Buller and Richard Herbert. The family claim descent from Lord Herbert of Cherbury, which claim is supported by the arms and crest engraved on the tombstone, they being the same as those borne by Sir Richard Herbert of Colbrooke, Monmouth, the youngest brother of William, first Earl of Pembroke. It is probable that Richard Herbert, citizen of London, is the same Richard mentioned in the Visitation of London, 1633.

LUNSFORD. Middlesex county.

Arms: Azure, a chevron between three boars' heads or, couped gules.

Crest. A boar's head or, couped gules.

Sir Thomas Lunsford, Knt. (28 Dec., 1641), came to Virginia in 1649, and on the 24 Oct., 1650, received a grant for 3,423 acres of land on the south side of Rappahannock River. He was a Lieut-Genl. of the Colony and member of the Council. He died ante 1656. He was married three times, his first wife being Catherine, daughter of Sir Henry Neville of Berkshire, by whom he had two daughters, and probably a son, William, the latter, it is thought, being the William Lunsford, Esq., who is mentioned as being one of the headrights in the grant to Sir Thomas in 1650. Sir Thomas married, 3rdly, Elizabeth, widow of Richard Kempe, late Secretary of State for Virginia. After Lunsford's death she married Maj.-Genl. Robert Smith of Middlesex county. By Lunsford she had a daughter Catherine, who married, 1st, Peter Jennings, Attorney-General, and, 2nd, about 1672, Ralph Wormeley, Secretary of State. She died 17 of May, 1685, leaving issue by Wormeley: (1) Elizabeth, married John Lomax and left issue; (2) Catherine, married Gawin Corbin, but left no issue.

GRAY. Stafford county.

Armes: Gules, a lion rampant within a bordure engrailed argent.

Crest: An anchor in pale or.

Motto: Anchor, fast anchor.

William Gray of Garlcraig, Scotland, married in 1718, Janet Barrie. His son, William Gray, also of Garlcraig, born 1729, died 1777, married Isabella, only child and heiress of John Bowie of "Hill of Bath" and Agnes Spreul, his wife. Their son, John Gray, born 4 March, 1769, at Garlcraig, came to America in 1784, and in 1809 purchased "Travellers' Rest," Stafford county, once the residence of Col. Burgess Ball. An old seal, brought to America by John Gray with the above arms engraved upon it, had once been the property of his grandfather, William Gray. It is now in the possession of his great grandson, John Bowie Gray of Stafford county.

HANSFORD. Gloucester county.

Arms: Sable, a star of eight rays argent.

Crest: On a chapeau gules, turned up ermine, a wyvern of the first, wings expanded argent.

The will of John Handford of Ludlowe, County Salop, Esqr. 17 Sept., 1669, probated 24 Jan., 1669-70 (P. C. C. Penn. 6), leaves certain estates contingently to "Tobias Handford, Gent., now living in Virginia, one of the sons of Hugh Handford, late of London, deceased, and then to his eldest sons in succession, and in case my said son and the said Tobias decease without issue, to Walter Handford of Wollashall, County Worcester."

The name of Handford was spelled indifferently Hansford, Hanford or Handford. The Hanfords of Wollashall, Worcestershire, had several branches of the family in London, and it is evident that Hugh Handford, deceased, was a member of the family. His son Tobias Handsford, named in thte above will, lived in Gloucester county, Va. On 8 Jan., 1666, Tobias Hansford received a grant of 324 acres in Ware Parish. On 24 Oct., 1673, he, together with Philip Ludwell and Richard Whitehead, received a grant of 20,000 acres in New Kent county.

LLOYD. Norfolk county.

 Arms: Azure, a lion rampant or.

 Crest: A demi lion rampant guardant or, supporting in the paws an arrow in pale argent.

 Cornelius Lloyd was a Lieut.-Col. of Militia in Lower Norfolk county in 1641, and a member of the House of Burgesses between 1642 and 1653. His wife was Elizabeth ————. Her will is dated 19 Feb., 1656-7, probated 15 June, 1657, in London. In it she describes herself as widow of Elizabeth River, Lower Norfolk county, Va. Cornelius Lloyd was a brother of Edward Lloyd of "Wye House," Maryland. This connection being established by a deed in 1655 from Elizabeth, the widow of Col. Cornelius Lloyd to Philemon Lloyd, son of her brother-in-law Edward Lloyd of Maryland, and in which she conveys to him certain personal estate. Edward Lloyd was born in Wales about 1600, came to Virginia in 1623, and was a member of the House of Burgesses 1637-49, removing in the latter year to Maryland with his wife, who was Alice Crouch and his son, Philemon. He was one of the original founders of Providence, afterward called Annapolis. He died in London, Eng., in 1696. The above arms are engraved upon numerous pieces of silver plate in the possession of his descendants and are also on the tomb of his son Philemon Lloyd, who married Henrietta Maria Neale, widow of Hon. Richard Bennett, and dau. of Capt. James Neale and Ann, his wife, who was Maid of Honour to Queen Henrietta Maria, wife of Charles I. Philemon Lloyd died 22 June, 1685, and the Lloyd arms impaling Bennett are on their tombs at "Wye House."

COKE. Williamsburg.

 Arms: Gules, three crescents and a canton or.

 Crest: The sun in splendour or.

 Motto: Non aliunde pendere.

 John Coke, who settled in Williamsburg in 1724, is identified by his letters and receipts for legacies preserved by the English branch of the family. His wife was Sarah Hoge, as shown in his will, proved 16 Nov., 1767, in which she is named and his two sons Samuel and Robie Coke. John Coke was descended from the Cokes of Trusley, Derbyshire, through Sir Francis Coke. Richard Coke, born 9 Nov., 1664, died 1730, married Elizabeth, daughter of Thomas Robie of Donnington, County Lincoln, and their third son,

John, born 6 Apr., 1704, settled in Williamsburg in 1724 (For English pedigree see Cokes of Trusley, County Derby).

MASON. Stafford county.

Arms: Per fesse embattled azure and argent on the embattlement a dove, wings expanded argent, beaked and legged gules; in base three fleurs de lis of the last, two and one.

Crest: A talbot passant reguardant, argent, eared sable, holding in the mouth a hart's horn or.

Motto: Pro Republica Semper.

Col. George Mason was a native of Stratford-on-Avon, Warwickshire, and came to Virginia about 1651. He was Sheriff of Stafford in 1659 and member of the House of Burgesses in 1676, also Colonel of Militia. He died 1686. A record in Westmoreland county, dated 1655, gives his wife's name as Mary. His numerous descendants were distinguished in the later history of the Colony. Col. George Mason, of "Gunston," about the year 1784, sent to London to have the above arms engraved upon the Mason silver, "together with those of Thompson of Yorkshire quartered therewith." (Mason Letters.)

DORMER. James River.

Arms: Azure, ten billets 4, 3, 2 and 1 or; on a chief of the second a demi lion rampant issuant sable.

Crest: A falconer's right hand glove fessewise argent, thereon perched a falcon, wings inverted, also argent, belled and beaked or.

Sir Fleetwood Dormer, Bart., of Arle Court, Gloucestershire, emigrated to Virginia (Burke's Extinct Baronetage). By a deed dated 26 Dec., 1649, John White of James Parish in Virginia sold 1,000 acres of land adjoining that of Fleetwood Dormer, Gent. Sir Fleetwood Dormer was the son of Sir Fleetwood Dormer, Bart., of Lee Grange, and Purton, County Bucks.

LUCKIN. Williamsburg.

Arms: Sable, a fesse indented between two leopards' faces or.

Crest: A demi griffin or, issuing out of a tower, paly of six of the last and sable.

The above arms (impaling those of Page) are engraved on the tomb of Alice Page, wife of Col. John Page of York county. She was Alice Luckin of Essex, Eng., born 1625, married 1656, died 22 June, 1698. Her tomb is in Bruton churchyard.

HOOKE. Elizabeth City.

Arms: Quarterly argent and sable, a cross between four escallops all counterchanged.

Crest: An escallop sable between two wings argent.

Capt. Francis Hooke was a naval officer, and on the 18th of Jan., 1636-7, was a member of the Council. He was dead in 1640, for at a Quarter Court, held at Jamestown April, 1640, Capt. Thomas Willoughby represented that he had furnished a barrel of gunpowder to accommodate the funeral of Capt. Francis Hooke, the late Commander of the Fort at Point Comfort. In Berry's Hampshire Genealogies, we find a pedigree of the family of Hooke, which is doubtless that from which Capt. Hooke descended, namely: (1) Richard Hooke of Surrey, married ——— Payne, of Eaton, and was the grandfather of John Hooke of Branshott, County Southampton, the latter having issue: (1) Henry of Branshott, and (2) Francis Hooke, Captain in R. N. 1634.

LINDSAY. Northumberland county.

Arms: Quarterly 1st and 4th, gules a fesse chequy, argent and azure; 2nd and 3rd, or a lion rampant gules, the shield debruised of a ribbon in bend sable over all.

Crest: A cubit arm in armor in pale, holding in the hand a sword erect argent, on the point a pair of balances of the last.

Motto: Recta sed ardua.

The Rev. David Lindsay of Yeocomico, Northumberland county, was the eldest son of Sir Hierome Lindsay, Knt., of "The Mount," Lyon King of Arms of Scotland, and his wife, Margaret Colville. An entry in the South Leith Church records shows that he was baptized 2 Jan., 1603. His broken tombstone, with portions of the above arms upon it, states that he died 3 Apr., 1667. His will was probated in Northumberland county, his wife being Susanna ———. His only daughter, Helen, married Capt. Thomas Opie, and their son, Capt. Thomas Opie, Jr., died 16 Nov., 1702, and was buried with his grandfather, the Rev. David Lindsay.

HOLFORD. Charles City county.

Arms: Argent a greyhound passant sable, a canton sable for difference.

In Omerod's History of Cheshire, vol. 2, p. 239, is the following pedigree of Holford of Davenham: (1) Arthur Holford, younger son of Sir George Holford of Holford; (2) Arthur of Davenham, Gent., living 6th Edward VI., married Anne, daughter of William Bostock of Huxley; (3) John of Davenham, Gent., born there 29 March, 1587-8, married Eleanor, daughter of Richard Hussey of Albright-Hussey, Salop; (4) John of Davenham, married Elizabeth, daughter of Thomas Reddish, Gent.; (5) John of Davenham, married Jane, daughter of Thomas Mallory, Dean of Chester, and had issue: (1) John, son and heir; (2) Richard; (3) Thomas Holford, married and in Virginia.

On 29 May, 1668, a patent for 5,878 acres in Charles City county, was granted to Thomas and Henry Batte, sons of Mr. John Batte, deceased, (whose wife was Martha, daughter of Thomas Mallory, Dean of Chester, and whose sister, Catherine, had married the Rev. Philip Mallory, a son of the Dean and afterwards a prominent minister in Virginia). Among the headrights for this patent are several persons named Batte, and Mallory, as well as Thomas and Anne Holford. This Thomas was, undoubtedly, the son of John and Jane Holford of Davenham.

CUSTIS. Northampton county.

Arms: Argent three popinjays vert.

Crest: An archer ppr. coat vert, shooting an arrow from a bow of the first.

The immigrant ancestor of this family was John Custis of Rotterdam, who was in Virginia in 1640. He had six sons: (1) Thomas of Baltimore, Ireland; (2) Edward of London; (3) Robert of Rotterdam, who was a tavern keeper there and whose daughter married about 1649 Argall Yardley, a son of the Virginia Governor; (4) John of Virginia; (5) William of Virginia; (6) Joseph of Virginia. John Custis, son of the immigrant, was Sheriff of Northampton in 1664, and Major-General of Militia in 1676. His estate, "Arlington," gave its name to the celebrated Custis estate near Washington. The family was originally from Gloucester county, Eng. The will of John Smithier of Arlington, County Gloucester, dated 16 Feb., 1618, probated 31 Oct., 1626, mentions his cousin "Henry Custis, alias Cliffe, son-in-law Edward Custis, alias Cliffe, and his son, John Custis; also William Custis, Nicholas Custis, etc." The tomb of John Custis at Northampton county bears the above arms (without the crest); stating he was one of the Council and Major-General of Virginia, and that he died 29 Jan., 1696, aged 66 years. The tomb of John Custis, grandson of the above, is also at "Arlington," and bears the Custis arms. The latter's will was dated Nov. 14, 1749, and probated in London 19 Nov., 1753. In it he desires "that he be interred by the side of his grandfather, under a white marble tombstone, engraved with his arms of 'three parrots.'" He was born in 1678, and married Frances Parke. The arms adopted by the Custis family were those of Cliffe of the county of Essex, Eng.

MILNER. Nansemond county.

Arms: Per pale or and sable, a chevron between three horses' bits, counterchanged.

Crest: A horse's head, couped argent, bridled and maned or.

Col. Thomas Milner was in Nansemond county 1675. He was Clerk of the House of Burgesses 1681-4, and Speaker of the same 1691-3. He married Mary ————, and his daughter Mary, born 6 Aug., 1667, married Col. Miles Cary, of "Richneck," Warwick county, and died 27 Oct., 1700. Upon her tomb are the above arms, which are those of Milner of Yorkshire. Col. Milner was deceased in 1694. His grandson, Thomas Milner, married in 1719, Mary, daughter of Samuel Selden and Rebecca, his wife. (Elizabeth City Records.)

HEYMAN. Elizabeth City.

Arms: Argent, on a chevron engrailed azure, between three martlets sable, as many cinquefoils or.

Crest: A Moor full faced, wreathed around the temples, holding in the dexter hand a rose slipped and leaved all ppr.

Peter Heyman was appointed one of the Deputy Postmaster Generals 18 Apr., 1692, and one of the Commissioners of the Customs in 1699. He was killed 29 Apr., 1700, on board the King's ship "Shoreham," which was engaged in a fight with a pirate. His tomb, at "Pembroke," near Hampton, bears the above arms, and it also states that he was a grandson of Sir Peter Heyman of Summerfield, county Kent, Eng.

TIMSON. York county.

Samuel Timson was in Virginia in 1677. He was a Justice in 1683 and subsequent years; died 23 Jan., 1694-5, and married Mary Juxon, sister of William Juxon, Gent., of London. She died 10 Oct., 1702, and they had issue: William, John, Samuel and Mary Timson. The tomb of Samuel Timson, the immigrant, is at Queen's Creek, York county, and bears the Timson arms impaling Juxon, namely: In the dexter for Juxon "Or, a cross gules between four blackamoors' heads, couped at the shoulders ppr. wreathed about the temples of the field." Sinister for Timson: charges much defaced, but representing "in chief two fleurs de lis, in base a sun in glory."

The arms in the sinister quarter bear no resemblance to those of Timson given in any of the English authorities.

HUME. Culpepper county.

Arms: Vert, a lion rampant argent, armed and langued gules.
Crest: A unicorn's head and neck argent, gorged with a coronet, maned and horned or.
Motto: Remember.

George Hume, the head of the house of Wedderburn, died in 1720. He married 4 Oct., 1695, Margaret, daughter of Sir Patrick Hume of Lumsden, by whom he had: (1) David d.s.p. 1764; (2) George; (3) Patrick; (4) Francis; (5) John; (6) James; (7) Margaret; (8) Jane. George Hume, the second son, was born at Wedderburn, Berwickshire, 30 May, 1697, and came to Culpepper in 1721. He married in 1728 Elizabeth Proctor of Fredericksburg, and died 1760, leaving issue: (1) George; (2) Francis; (3) John; (4) William; (5) James; (6) Charles. The last person to bear the title of Earl of Marchmont was Alexander Hume Campbell. He married Lady Arabella, daughter and co-heir of Philip, 2nd Earl of Hardwick. But dying in 1781 d.s.p., the honor died with him. The title of right, belongs to the Virginia family of Humes (See House of Lords Sessions Papers 1822, and the same for 1838).

GRYMES. Middlesex county.

Arms: Or, a bordure engrailed azure on a chief sable three escallops argent.
Crest: A pair of wings addorsed or.

The Rev. Charles Grymes of Gloucester and York counties, had a son John, who married Alice, daughter of Laurence and Sarah Townley. The latter was a daughter of Col. Augustine Warner, Sr., of "Warner Hall." John Grymes died 28 Aug., 1709, aged 69 years. His eldest son, Hon. John Grymes of "Brandon," Middlesex, was born in 1693, died 2 Nov., 1749. He was Burgess for Middlesex 1718, Auditor-General 1716, and member of the Council in 1725. He married Lucy, daughter of Philip Ludwell of Greensprings. Frequent mention of the Grymes family is contained in the Parish Register of Christ Church, Middlesex. The will of John Grymes, 2nd, dated 1747, bears a wax seal with the above arms. According to Burke, these are the arms of Grimes of Bonchurch, Isle of Wight, Eng.

Charles Grymes, the immigrant, patented land in Lancaster county in 1653 and 1654, and in 1657 there are three patents to Charles Grimes, Clerk.

DUNCOMBE. Lancaster county.

Arms: A chevron between three buglehorns.

Crest: On an esquire's helmet, a stag's head.

The above arms are on a wax seal on the will of Thomas Duncombe, probated at Lancaster Court House 1659. They are not credited to the name of Duncombe by any of the English authorities. On the 24th of July, 1635, a Joseph Duncomb, aged 46, embarked for Virginia on the ship "Assurance." (Hotten.)

HILL. Charles City county.

Arms: A lion passant.

Crest: A demi lion.

Col. Edward Hill of "Shirley," Charles City county, was a member of the House of Burgesses between the years 1639-54. He was Speaker of the House in 1644-54, and member of the Council from 1654. He died about 1663. His son, Col. Edward Hill, 2nd, was born 1637, died 30 Nov., 1700, and was Commander-in-Chief of Charles City and Surry counties, Attorney-General 1679; member of the Council, Treasurer and Speaker of the House of Burgesses, and in 1697 was Judge of the Admiralty Court for Virginia and North Carolina. He had issue: (1) Col. Edward Hill, 3rd, of "Shirley," d.s.p.; (2) Elizabeth, married in 1723 John Carter of "Corotoman," Lancaster county, and inherited "Shirley"; (3) Martha, married Hugh Gifford of Devonshire, Eng. The tomb of the second Col. Edward Hill at "Shirley" bears the above arms, but the tinctures are not designated. The arms of Hill of the county of Wexford, Ireland, contain a lion passant, with a demi lion passant for a crest.

JONES. Frederick county.

Arms: Argent, a lion rampant vert, vulned in the breast gules.

Crest: The sun in splendour or.

Arms taken from a book plate of Gabriel Jones of Frederick county, born 17 May, 1724, died 1806, the son of John Jones of Montgomery county, Wales, and Elizabeth, his wife, who came to Virginia in 1720. His mother was born 1689, and died 1st Jan., 1745. Gabriel Jones was King's Attorney for Augusta county. He married 16 Oct., 1749, Margaret, daughter of William Strother of King George county, and widow of George Morton, by whom he had issue: (1) Margaret, married Col. John Harvie; (2) Eliza-beth, third wife of John Lewis of Fredericksburg; (3) a daughter, married John Hawkins of Kentucky; (4) William Strother Jones, married Frances Thornton, widow of Dr. Horace Buckner of Culpeper.

YEARDLEY. Northampton county.
Arms: Argent on a chevron azure, three garbs or, on a canton gules a fret or.
Crest: A buck courant gules attired or.
Sir George Yeardley came to Virginia in 1609, and was Deputy-Governor in 1616-7. He was knighted in 1618, being appointed Governor of Virginia in that year. He was again appointed Governor in 1626, and held the office until his death in Nov., 1627, being buried on the 13th of that month. He married Temperance ————, and had issue: (1) Col. Argall Yeardley, born 1605, member of the Council 1644-5, married about 1650 to Sarah, daughter of John Custis of Northampton county, and died 1670, while Sheriff. His son Argall was in Northampton in 1670; (2) Col. Francis Yeardley of Northampton, afterward of Lower Norfolk county, was, in 1652, a member of the Maryland Council, but returned to Virginia and was Burgess of Lower Norfolk in 1655. He married Sarah, widow of Capt. John Gookin and d.s.p.; (3) Elizabeth Yeardley, born 1603.

SPOTSWOOD. Spotsylvania county.
Arms: Argent a chevron gules between three oak trees eradicated vert.
Crest: An eagle rising gules, looking to the sun in its splendour.
Motto: Patior ut potiar.
Gov. Alexander Spotswood was a great grandson of John Spotswood of Spotswood, Scotland, who, in 1635, became Archbishop of Glasgow and one of the Privy Council. His grandfather, Sir Robert, was president of the Court of Sessions. His father, Dr. Robert Spotswood, married Catherine Elliott, a widow, and their only child, Alexander, was born in 1070, at Tangiers. He fought under Marlborough at Blenheim, and became Governor of Virginia, being removed from that office in Sept., 1722. In 1720 he was Deputy Postmaster-General of America, and in 1740 was appointed Major-General of an expedition against Carthagena, but died before the embarkation at Annapolis, June 7 of that year. He married Ann Butler, and had issue, four children.

ISHAM. Henrico county.
Arms: Gules, three piles wavy or, over all a fesse of the second.
Henry Isham was in Virginia in 1656 and was a nephew of Sir Edward Brett of Blendenhall, Kent. He married Katherine, widow of Joseph Royall of Henrico, and died about 1675. There is a deed in Henrico, dated 23 Sept., 1678, to Henry Isham of London, merchant, only son and executor of Henry Isham of Virginia,

Gent., deceased. The will of Henry Isham, Jr., is at Henrico, dated 13 Nov., 1678, probated 1 Feb., 1678-9. In it he mentions "his half-brother, Joseph Royall, his honored mother, Mrs. Katherine Isham, his sister, Mrs. Ann Isham, his sister, Mrs. Mary Randolph." Mrs. Katherine Isham's will is dated 10 Aug., 1686, and probated in Dec. of that year. Attached to a paper at Henrico is an impression in wax of the above arms.

LUDLOW. York county.

Arms: Argent a chevron between three martins' heads erased sable.

Crest: A demi martin rampant sable.

Motto: Omne solum forte patria.

Col. George Ludlow, born at Denton, Wilts, 15 Sept., 1596, obtained a patent 26 July, 1646, for 1,452 acres in York county. His will being probated there 1st of Aug., 1656. He left his property to his nephew, Lieut.-Col. Thomas Ludlow, son of Gabriel and Phillis Ludlow. Thomas was baptized in Warminster 1st of Nov., 1624, and John Ludlow, his brother, qualified upon his estate in Virginia 20 Dec., 1660. (An extended pedigree of the English branch of the family is in New England Hist. & Gen. Register, vol. 24, pp. 181-84.)

STONE. Accomac county.

Arms: Per pale or and sable, a lion rampant counterchanged.

Capt. William Stone of Hungers Creek was born in Northampton, Eng., in 1603, and came to Virginia about 1633. He was a nephew of Thomas Stone, merchant, of London (the uncle's descent is given in the Visitation of London, 1633-5). In 1635 Capt. Stone was a Justice of Accomac, and in 1640 Sheriff of Northampton county. He removed to Maryland, and died about 1695 at his manor of "Avon," in Charles county. He was commissioned Governor of Maryland in 1648 by Lord Baltimore. An old ring, now in the possession of a descendant of Gov. Stone, has engraven upon it the arms as above given. In his will the Governor mentions his brothers, Richard and Matthew, brother Sprigg and sons, Thomas, Richard, John and Matthew; and daughters, Elizabeth, Catherine and Mary.

WEST. Northumberland county.

Arms: Argent, on a fesse dancette sable, three leopards' faces jessant de lis.

Anthony West came to Virginia in the "James'" 1622 (Hotten). His will is dated 12 Oct., 1651, probated 5 May, 1652. By his wife, Ann, he had issue, a daughter, Katherine, and a son, Lieut.-Col. John West of Northumberland county, who married Matilda Scarburgh, and had issue, six sons and several daughters. At Onancock, Accomac county, is the tomb of Major Charles West, a grandson of John West. He died 28 Feb., 1757, and upon the slab is engraven the above arms.

RICH. Gloucester county.

Arms: For arms, see Willis of York and Gloucester counties.

LUKE. Westmoreland county.

Arms: Argent, a buglehorn sable, stringed gules.

George Luke, son of Oliver Luke of Woodend, Bedfordshire, settled in Westmoreland county, and married Mrs. Smith, the widowed sister of William Fitzhugh. George Luke died in 1732 and is buried at Cople Church, Bedfordshire. The inscription on the tomb states, "He was the last Luke of Woodend." He was descended from Sir Walter Luke of Cople, Judge of the King's Bench. His father, Oliver Luke, married Elizabeth, daughter of Onslow Winch of Bedfordshire, and George, their fourth child, was born 29 July, 1659.

MORYSON. Elizabeth City county.

Arms: Argent, on a cross sable, five fleurs de lis or; in dexter quarter a martlet azure.

Major Richard, Lieut. Robert and Col. Francis Moryson, successively commanded the Fort at Point Comfort. They were sons of Sir Richard Moryson of Tooley Park, Leicestershire, and his wife, Elizabeth, daughter of Sir Henry Harrington. Major Richard Moryson commanded Point Comfort 1638, and in 1641 was member of the Council. His will is dated 1626, probated 27 Dec., 1648. He had two sons, Richard, d.s.p., and Charles, who married Rebecca, executrix of Col. Leonard Yeo. She afterward married Col. John Lear of Nansemond. Charles Moryson in 1680 was Lieut.-Col. and a Magistrate of Elizabeth City. He died 1688. Lieut. Robert Moryson commanded Point Comfort in 1641. He married Jane ————, and d.s.p. 25 Oct., 1647. Col. Francis Moryson came to Virginia in 1649 and was captain of the Fort at Point Comfort. He was Speaker of the House of Burgesses and Acting Governor. He returned to England and left issue.

RING. York county.

Arms: Argent, on a bend gules, three crescents of the first.

Crest: A hand vested sable cuffed or, holding a roll of paper.

Joseph Ring, merchant, of York county, born 1646, died 26 Feb., 1702-3, and the above arms are upon his tomb. He lived at "Ringfield," Felgates Creek, and was a Burgess for York in 1691. The original house which he built is still standing.

WILLIS. York and Gloucester counties.

Arms: Argent, three griffins passant sable, a bordure engrailed gules bezantee.

Francis Willis was born in the Parish of St. Fowles alias St. Algate, Oxford. He was a Magistrate of York county, Va., in 1648, member of the House of Burgesses from Gloucester 1652, 1658-9; Counsellor 1658-75, with title of Colonel. He died in England in 1689, his will being probated 25 Apr., 1691. He left his estates on Ware Creek, Gloucester county, to his nephew, Francis, son of his brother, Henry Willis, deceased. Francis Willis, 2nd, had two sons, Francis Willis, 3rd, of Ware Parish, and Henry Willis, founder of Fredericksburg. Francis Willis, 3rd, married Anne Rich, daughter of Edward and niece of Elias Rich of St. Paul, Covent Garden, the latter's will being probated in London 11 Feb., 1719. Anne Rich was born in 1696, and died 10 June, 1727. Her tombstone describing her as the wife of Col. Francis Willis, is in the chancel of Ware Church, Gloucester, and bears the above described arms of Willis, impaling Rich, the latter being, "Gules, a chevron between three crosses botonnee or."

KING. Nansemond county.

Arms: Or, three pheons.

Michael King was in Virginia previous to 1694, for in that year there is recorded a grant to Michael King, Jr., and William King for 340 acres in Nansemond county, and there is also a grant of 443 acres in the same county in the year 1716 to John King, son of Michael King. Miles King descended from Michael, was born 2 Nov., 1747, died in Norfolk 19 June, 1814. He was Surgeon's Mate in First Virginia Regiment, Oct. 26, 1775. Member of the House of Delegates 1784, 1791-3 and 1798. Mayor of Norfolk 1804-05 and again in 1810. His book plate, bearing the above arms, is found in two books now in the Library of William and Mary College. The arms are somewhat similar to those of King, Earl Lovelace, in whose coat are found "Sable three spear heads erect argent, embrued gules."

MANN. Gloucester county.

Arms: Per fesse embattled counter embattled argent and azure, three goats passant counterchanged attired or.

Arms on the tomb at Timber Neck, Gloucester county, of Mary Mann, who died 18 March, 1703-4, aged 56. Along side of it is the tomb of her husband, John Mann, who died 7 Jan., 1694, aged 63 years. Mary Mann was the widow of Edmund Berkeley. The will of John Mann, her second husband, was proved in Gloucester county 13 Feb., 1694. The arms on the tomb are similar to those of Mann of the counties of Kent and Norfolk.

PAWLETT. Henrico county.

Arms: Sable, three swords in pile, points in base argent, pommelled and hilted or, between two flanges of the last pellettee.

Crest: On a mount, a falcon rising or, pellettee, belled of the last.

Capt. Thomas Pawlet, born 1578, and brother of John, first Lord Pawlet, came to Virginia in 1618, and in 1625 lived at Westover. In 1631-2 he was a Justice, and in 1641 Member of the Council. He died 1644 without issue, leaving his estate of Westover to his brother Lord Pawlet, whose son sold the property to Theodoric Bland in 1665.

SPELMAN.

Arms: Sable, twelve plates between two flaunches argent.

Crest: A wild man ppr.

Capt. Henry Spelman was the third son of the celebrated antiquarian, Sir Henry Spelman of Narburgh, Norfolk. He came to Virginia in 1609, when about 21 years of age, and was killed by the Indians in 1623.

WEST. New Kent county.

Arms: Argent, a fesse dancettee sable.

Crest: Out of a ducal coronet or, a griffin's head azure ears and beak gold.

Motto: Jour de ma vie.

John West, brother of Thomas, third Lord Delaware, was Governor of Virginia 1635-7, member of the Council and House of Burgesses, also Justice of York county. He died 1659-60 and married Anne ———, by whom he had John, his only son and heir, of West Point, King William county. The latter was Colonel and Justice of New Kent county in 1680, and died 1689. He married Ursula, daughter of Major Joseph Croshaw of York county, and had issue: John, Nathaniel, Thomas and a daughter, Anne, who married Henry Fox.

JONES. Prince George county.

Arms: Per bend sinister ermine and ermines, a lion rampant or a bordure engrailed of the last.

Crest: A lion's head erased.

The above arms are engraved on the hilt of a sword worn by Major Cadwallader Jones of Prince George county, when a captain in Baylor's Regiment, and aide de camp to Lafayette. It descended to his grandson, Col. Cadwallader Jones, who wore it during the Civil War as Colonel of the 12th South Carolina Volunteers, Greggs' Brigade.

PEACHEY. Richmond county.

Arms: Azure, a lion rampant double queued ermine, ducally crowned or, a canton of the last charged with a mullet pierced gules.

Crest: A demi lion double queued ermine, holding in the dexter paw a sword, point upward.

Samuel Peachey, the immigrant, was the son of Robert Peachey of Milden Hall, Suffolk, and Anne Hodgskin, his wife. He was a Justice of Richmond county and in 1704 a Lieut.-Col. His will, dated 29 Jan., 1711, probated 4 June, 1712, leaves large legacies to his nephews and nieces, the sons and daughters of Nathaniel Peachey. He also mentions his grandson, Samuel Peachey, to whom he leaves, "My great silver tankard and my sealed ring, having both my coate of Armes."

MAYO. Henrico county.

Arms: Gules, chevron vair, between three ducal coronets or, a crescent for difference.

Crest: A unicorn's head erased, charged with a chevron vair.

Arms on the tomb at Powhatan of Joseph Mayo, Gent., born in Somersetshire 25 March, 1693, died 25 March, 1740, also on the tomb of George Mayo, eldest son of above, born in the Isle of Barbadoes 30 Aug., 1717, died 19 Feb., 1739. Joseph Mayo emigrated from the Isle of Barbadoes to Virginia about 1727, and resided at Powhatan, near Richmond.

FLOURNOY. Henrico county.

Arms: D'azur au chevron d'argent accompagne en chef de deux fleurs ou chatons de noyer d'or, et un pointe d'une noix de meme.

Motto: Ex flore fructus.

The Flournoy or Flournois family are descended from the Flournoys who fled from Champagne to Geneva, Switzerland, after the massacre of the Huguenots at Vassy in 1562. The Virginia family trace from Jacob Flournoy, who had land in Henrico in 1705, and from his nephew, Jean Jacques Flournoy, born 17 Nov., 1686, married in Va. 23 June, 1720, to Elizabeth, daughter of James Williams, by whom he had issue, ten children. The pedigree of the Virginia Flournoys is as follows: (1) Laurent Flournoy, married Gabrielle Mellin of Lyons; (2) Jean Flournoy, born 1574, married Frances Musard; (3) Jacques Flournoy, born 1608, married Judith Pucrary; (4) Jacques Flournoy, born 1657, married Julia Eyraud and were the parents of Jean Jacques Flournoy of Va. Jacob Flournoy, uncle of Jean Jacques, was born 5 Jan., 1663, and was a son of Jacques and Judith Pucrary Flournoy (as above). He came to Va. in 1700 and settled near Williamsburg, bringing with him his 2nd wife and sons, Francis and Jacques, and a daughter, Jane Frances. The Virginia and the Geneva branches of the family, together with the arms, are established through the family records of Mr. Edmond Flournoy of Geneva, who is the owner of a manuscript pedigree of the various branches of the name, which was begun in 1732.

PEARSON. Stafford county.

Arms: Per fess embattled azure and gules, three suns or.

According to the "Bland Pedigree," Thomas Pierson of Wisbeach, Isle of Ely, gent., married Susanna Bland, born about 1617, sister of Theodorick Bland of Westover. They had a son Thomas, who had Thomas Pierson of Stafford county, Va., who had Simon Pearson of the same county, whose will is dated 7 Dec., 1731, probated 16 Nov., 1733. He had issue: (1) Constantia, born 1714, married Nathaniel Chapman (see Chapman of Stafford); (2) Susanna, born 29 Dec., 1717, married John Alexander 11 Dec., 1743, died 6 Oct., 1788; (3) Thomas, will proved 18 May, 1744, and who had issue; (4) Margaret, born 5 March, 1720, married, 1st, 27 Jan., 1735, William Henry Terrett, 2nd, John West. Her will was proved 10 Jan., 1798.

LEWIS. Gloucester county.

Arms: Quarterly. (1) Argent a dragon's head and neck erased vert, holding in the mouth a bloody hand (Lewis). 2. Gules three towers triple towered argent (Howell). 3. Argent three chevronels. (Not identified.) 4. Argent three torteaux. (Not identified.) 5. Argent a chief azure three lozenges or. (Fielding.) 6. Vert a cross engrailed or. (Warner.) 7. Azure three bowls argent, out of each a boar's head or. (Bowles).

Crest: Argent a dragon's head and neck erased vert, holding in the mouth a bloody hand.

The above arms are from silver plate in the possession of the Lewis family, the quarterings denoting the various intermarriages. The printed pedigrees of the family are many, and varied in their conclusions as to the first of the Lewis name in Virginia. It is extremely probable that he was the "Mr. John Lewis" who patented 22 April, 1668, land in Gloucester and New Kent counties. According to the tombstone of his son, Col. John Lewis, he married Isabella ————, and had issue, John Lewis of Warner Hall, and probably other children.

MARTIN. Caroline county.

Arms: Gules a chevron between three crescents argent.

Arms of Colonel John Martin of Caroline county, engraved on a silver pint cup, and advertised by him as "stolen" in the Virginia Gazette of 20 Nov., 1738.

Colonel Martin was a member of the House of Burgesses for the above county in 1738 and 1740, and from King William county 1752 to 1756. He died in the latter year. At Clifton, Caroline county, is the tomb of his wife, the epitaph states that she was Martha, daughter of Lewis Burwell, Esq., of Gloucester county, and that she died 27 May, 1738, aged 36 years, leaving three sons and four daughters.

METCALFE. Richmond county.

Arms: Argent three calves passant sable.

Crest: A talbot sejant ppr. dexter paw grasping a golden target.

Richard Metcalfe of Rappahannock River, Va., 1708, was a son of Gilbert Metcalfe, merchant, of London, who traced descent from Richard Metcalfe of North Allerton, Yorkshire. (See Foster's Pedigrees of Yorkshire Families.)

METCALF. King William county.

Same arms as above.

Thomas Metcalf, son of Samuel Metcalf of Northwick, Cheshire, was born 10 Aug., 1734, and came to Virginia 16 May, 1751, with his uncle John Metcalf. He married 23 Nov., 1756, Elizabeth, born 13 Aug., 1734, the eldest daughter of John Strachey, M. D., of Sutton Court, Somersetshire, and by her had issue, six children, all of whom d.s.p. except a daughter, Ann Lee Metcalf, who married Dr. Claudius Levert.

RAE. Williamsburg.

Arms: Vert a chevron argent between three roebucks courant ppr.

Crest: A roebuck at gaze ppr.

Motto: Ever ready.

The above arms are engraved on the tomb in Bruton churchyard of Robert Rae, merchant of Falmouth; born 1723, died 30 May, 1753, the son of Robert Rae, Esq., of Little Govan, near Glasgow, Scotland.

THRUSTON. Norfolk county.

Arms: Sable three buglehorns argent stringed or, garnished azure.

Crest: A heron argent.

Motto: Esse quam videri.

The immigrant was Malachy Thruston, born 19 Jan., 1637, who was a lawyer in Virginia from 1670. His will, dated 14 March, 1698-9, probated 15 Nov. in Norfolk county, states, that "I leave to my son, John Thruston, my signett Ring with my coat of Armes." Malachy was the grandson of Malachias Thruston of Wellington, Somersetshire, born ante 1600, Malachias's wife died 1651. Their son John was born 8 June, 1606, at Wellington, and became Chamberlain of the City of Bristol. He died 8 April, 1675, and is buried at St. Thomas, Bristol. He was married twice, having by his first wife 16 children, and by the second, 8 children. Edward Thruston, brother of Malachy, the immigrant, came to Virginia ante 1666. He was born at Bristol 30 Jan., 1638, and married in Va. 28 Oct., 1666, Anne, daughter of Thomas Loveing, merchant, of Martin's Hundred. She died 17 Dec., 1670, and Edward married, 2nd, in Bristol 2 Aug., 1671, Susanna Perry, daughter of Nicholas Perry of Gt. Marlow. From 1680 to 1683 Edward Thruston resided at Ashton, Eng., at which place his wife died 2 Aug., 1683. He returned to Virginia in 1717, and has many descendants.

WALLACE. Elizabeth City.

Arms: Gules a lion rampant argent.

Crest: An ostrich head and neck ppr. holding a horseshoe in the beak or.

Arms on the tomb of the Rev. James Wallace, at "Erroll," Elizabeth City. He was born in Erroll, Perthshire, Scotland; minister in Elizabeth City for 21 years, and died 3 Nov., 1712, in his 45th year. He married, in 1695, Anne, daughter of John Sheppard and widow of Thomas Wythe (grandfather of George Wythe), and had issue: (1) Euphan, born 1696; (2) Ann, married Col. Robert Armistead; (3) James, member of the House of Burgesses 1769-72; (4) Mary; (5) John, died 1724.

PENDLETON. King and Queen county.

Arms: Gules an inescutcheon argent between four escallops in saltire or.

Crest: On a chapeau gules turned up ermine a demi dragon, wings inverted or, holding an escallop argent.

Motto: Maneo qualis manebam.

The Virginia Pendletons are descended from the ancient family of that name who were settled at Norwich, Norfolk, and originally from Manchester. George Pendleton removed from the latter city to Norwich in 1613, and married Elizabeth, daughter of John Pettingall, gent., of that city; they had a son, Henry, who married Susan ———+—, by whom a son, Henry, who had two sons, the Rev. Nathaniel Pendleton, who d.s.p., and Philip Pendleton, who came to Virginia in 1674. Philip was born about 1650, and married Isabella Hurt or Hart, by whom he had three sons and four daughters. His eldest son, Henry, born 1683, married, 1701, Mary, daughter of James Taylor of Caroline county by his second wife, Mary Gregory. He died 1721 and left issue: Philip, Nathaniel, John, Edmund, Mary and Isabella Pendleton.

MILLER. Prince George county.

Arms: Ermine three wolves heads erased gules.

Arms of Miller impaling Bolling, engraved upon a silver castor, once the property of Hugh Miller of Prince George. The Bolling arms being, "Sable an inescutcheon ermine within an orle of eight martlets argent."

Hugh Miller was a prominent merchant at Blandford and was the first master of the Blandford Lodge, F. and A. M., in 1757. He married Jane, daughter of Robert Bolling, Jr., and had issue: Anne, born 13 March, 1742-3; Robert, born 28 March, 1746; Jane, born 21 Feb., 1747-8; Lillias and Hugh.

Hugh Miller died 13 Feb., 1762, his will being proved at Somerset House, London, in March of that year. Two of the above daughters, Ann and Jane, became successively the wife of Sir Peyton Skipwith, Bart.

PERROTT. Middlesex county.

Arms: Three pears.

Richard Perrott, President of the Middlesex County Court, died 11 Nov., 1686. His son, Richard, born 24 Feb., 1657, was the first male child of English parentage born on the Rappahannock. He married 11 Feb., 1672, Sarah, born 16 Aug., 1657, widow of William Halfhide and daughter of Major Thomas Curtis and Averilla, his wife. They had issue: Henry, born 25 Jan., 1675; Frank, born 28 Aug., 1677; Sarah, born 21 Sept., 1679; Richard, born 5 Oct., 1681; Averilla, born 3 Aug., 1683; Robert, born 25 Oct., 1685; Curtis, born 19 Aug., 1688; Mary, born 19 Jan., 1690.

The arms of "3 pears" are on a seal of Richard Perrot at Middlesex Court House.

YUILLE. Williamsburg.

Arms: Argent on a fess between three crescents sable, a goat or, banded gules.

Crest: An ear of wheat ppr.

Motto: Numine et virtute.

Arms on the tomb of John Yuille, merchant, in Bruton church-yard. He died Oct., 1746, aged 27 years, and was the son of Thomas Yuille of Darleith, Scotland. These arms are ascribed by Burke to Yule of Darleith.

MENIFIE. James City county.

On a deed from George Menifie, dated 21 April, 1638, to Richard Kempe, there is a wax seal, bearing for device the trunk of a tree. (Ludwell MSS.)

George Menifie came to Virginia in 1625. He was Burgess for James City in 1629 and member of the Council 1635-46. His only child, Elizabeth, married Captain Henry Perry of Charles City county, member of the Council. They had two daughters, Elizabeth, who married John Coggs of Rainslip, Middlesex, and Mary, who married Thomas Mercer, stationer, of London. The will of George Menifie is dated 31 Dec., 1645, probated 25 Feb., 1646-7, in the Preg. Court of Canterbury. His wife, Mary, was alive at that time.

RAMSAY. Norfolk

Arms: Argent an eagle displayed sable, beaked and membered gules.

Crest: A unicorn's head couped argent, armed or.

Wax seal on the will of Dr. George Ramsay in clerk's office at Norfolk. Will dated 22 June, 1756. He devises his property to his wife, Sarah, and his sons, John and James Ramsay.

SHEILD. York county.

Arms: Gules on a bend engrailed or, three escutcheons sable.

Crest: A fleur de lis.

Motto: Be Traiste.

Robert Sheild of England and his wife, Elizabeth Bray, had Robert, to whom Edward Mihill in 1646 deeded two cows in York county. In 1661 Elizabeth Mihill, widow of said Edward, married Capt. William Hay of York county and made deed of gifts in which she "provided for her son Robert Sheild, whom she had by her first husband, Robert Sheild, and for her brother Arthur Bray of London, and her first husband's nephew, Thomas Sheild." The son, Robert Sheild, died 4 March, 1669-70. He married Elizabeth ————, and had issue, a son, Robert, who was born 26 April 1667, and married Mary, only daughter of Charles Dunn, by whom Elizabeth, born 18 Jan., 1690, died 29 Dec., 1692; Robert, born 18 April, 1693; Dunn, born 2 Jan., 1695, died 29 May, 1732; Anne, born 25 Jan., 1698, died 16 Oct., 1719; Thomas, born 12 April, 1702, died 11 Nov., 1732; John, born 19 April, 1706, died 7 Oct., 1734; Charles, born 12 April., 1709.

The Sheild arms are engraved on an old seal and also on old silver plate in the possession of descendants of the immigrant.

TARRANT. Essex county.

Arms: A lion rampant reguardant.

Crest: On an Esquire's helmet, a demi-lion rampant.

Wax seal on the will of Leonard Tarrant at Tappahannock, Essex county, dated 4 June, 1718.

No such arms are ascribed to Tarrant by the English authorities.

MOSELEY. Norfolk county.

Arms: Quarterly 1st and 4th. Sable a chevron between three battle axes argent; 2nd and 3rd. or a fess between three eagles displayed sable.

Crest: An eagle displayed sable.

Motto: Mos legem regit.

William Mosely settled in 1649 in Lower Norfolk county, where was built "Rolleston," named for the family seat of the Moseleys, Rolleston Hall, Staffordshire, the immigrant bringing with him a copy of his arms, and many family portraits. He was a Justice from 1649 to 1655. His will, dated 29 June, 1655, was probated 15 Aug. of the same year. He left a wife, Susanna, and sons, Arthur and William. The inventory of the wife's estate is dated 8 Feb., 1655-6. William Moseley, 2nd, died about 1671. He was Commissioner for Lower Norfolk in 1660. He married Mary, daughter of Capt. John Gookin, by his wife, Sarah Offley, the widow of Capt. Adam Thoroughgood, and she, after Capt. Gookin's death, married Francis, son of Sir George Yeardley. Mary (Gookin) Moseley, married, 2nd, in 1672, Lieut.-Col. Anthony Lawson. William Moseley, 2nd, had issue: William, John, Elizabeth and Edward. Edward Moseley, born in 1661, will probated 1736, was a Colonel and Justice of Princess Anne county, High Sheriff 1707-8, Knight of the Golden Horseshoe 1710-22, and member of the House of Burgesses. He married Mrs. Bartholomew Taylor, daughter of Col. John Stringer, and was the father of Hillary Moseley, to whom he gave 1 Feb., 1703-4, "My seale, which was my father's, with his coat of arms on it." Hillary died before his father, his will being probated 5 Aug., 1730. He married Hannah ————, and left a son Edward Hack Moseley.

TALMAN. New Kent county.

Arms: Gules a chevron in chief two daggers points downwards, in base a sword, point upward or.

Crest: An arm embowed in armor holding a battle axe all ppr.

Motto: In fide et in bello fortis.

Capt. Henry Talman of New Kent county, was the son of William Talman of Felmingham Hall, Wiltshire, gent., and grandson of Christopher Talman and Joanna, his wife. Captain Talman married Ann Elizabeth Ballard and died in London in 1775. The following entries concerning the family are from the St. Peter's register of New Kent: "Martha, dau. of Henry and Ann Talman, born 16 March, 1733, bapt. 16 June; Rebeckah, dau. of Henry and

Ann Talman, born 2 April, bapt. 12 June, 1737; Henry, son of Henry and Ann Talman, born 26 Dec., bapt. 8 April, 1739."

WARNER. York and Gloucester counties.

Arms: Vert, a cross engrailed or.

Col. Augustine Warner, born 28 Nov., 1610, died 24 Dec., 1674, came to Virginia in 1628. He was Justice of York 1652, and of Gloucester 1656, Burgess for York 1652, and for Gloucester 1658, and member of the Council 1659 until his death. He named his home in Gloucester "Warner Hall." He married Mary ————, who died 11 Aug., 1662, and had issue, Col. Augustine, 2nd, born 3 July, 1642, died 19 June, 1681. He was Speaker of the House of Burgesses 1675-7, and also a member of the Council. He married Mildred, daughter of Col. George Reade, and had issue, Augustine, born 17 Jan., 1666, died 17 March, 1686; George, born 1677 and d.s.p.; Mildred, married, first, Lawrence Washington of Westmoreland county and was the grandmother of George Washington. She married, secondly, George Gale and died in England in 1700; Elizabeth, born 24 Nov., 1672, died 5 Feb., 1719-20, married Col. John Lewis and inherited "Warner Hall"; Mary, married 17 Feb., 1680, John Smith of Purton and died 13 Nov., 1700. The arms are taken from old silver in possession of the descendants.

TAYLOE. York and Richmond counties.

Arms: Vert, a sword erect or, between two lions rampant addorsed ermine.

The first of the name in this country was Col. William Tayloe, who married Elizabeth Kingsmill (for her arms see under Kingsmill), and upon her tomb, recently removed to Norfolk, are the arms of Tayloe impaling Kingsmill. Col. Tayloe was Burgess and Counsellor of York county. He d.s.p., his heir being his nephew, Col. William Tayloe of Richmond county, who married Ann, fourth daughter of Henry Corbin. Col. Tayloe, 2nd, died 1711. His son, John Tayloe of Mount Airy, Richmond county, was born 5 Feb., 1697, died 1747, and married Elizabeth Fauntleroy. They had issue: John, born 28 May, 1721, married Rebecca, eldest daughter of George Plater, Esq., of St. Mary's county, Md., and had issue, a son, John, and nine other children, of whom eight were daughters and became the wives of Gov. Edward Lloyd of Maryland, Francis Lightfoot Lee, Ralph Wormeley, Thomas Lomax, Mann Page, Landon Carter, Robert Beverley and William Augustine Washington. The arms used by the family are those of Teylow of Bisley, Gloucestershire.

BACON. York county.

Arms: Argent, on a fesse engrailed between three escutcheons gules as many mullets argent pierced sable.

The above arms are upon the tomb of Col. Nathaniel Bacon, Sr., President of the Virginia Council, at Ringfield, York county. The Rev. James Bacon, rector of Burgate, Suffolk, died 25 Aug., 1670.

He was the second son of Sir James Bacon of Friston Hall, Suffolk. The Rev. James had issue, the above named Nathaniel, bapt. 29 Aug., 1620, died 16 March, 1692, and came to Virginia 1650. Col. Nathaniel married Elizabeth, daughter of Richard Kingsmill and widow of Col. William Tayloe. They had issue: (1) Martha, married Anthony Smith of Colchester; (2) Elizabeth, married Thomas Burrows of Bury, St. Edmunds; (3) Anne, married ———— Wilkinson of Burgate. The tomb of Col. Bacon's wife has been removed to St. Paul's churchyard, Norfolk. She died 2 Nov., 1691, in her 67th year. The tomb bears arms, "Argent crusilly, sable, a chevron ermines between three millrinds of the second, a chief of the third" (for Kingsmill), impaling "Vert a sword erect or between two lions rampant endorsed ermine" (for Tayloe).

ZOUCH. Henrico county.

Arms: Gules, bezantee a canton ermine.

Sir John Zouch of Codnor, Derbyshire, was Governor of Va. in 1631. He sold his estates in England and he and his son and daughters became residents of Virginia. His will, dated 30 Aug., 1636, probated 1639, mentions his son John, and his daughters, Isabella, Elizabeth and Mary.

LAWSON. Lancaster county.

Arms: A chevron between three martlets.

The first of this line was Rowland Lawson, whose will was probated 8 May, 1661, in Lancaster county. His children were: Rowland, Elizabeth, John, Henry and Letitia. On the 14th of Sept., 1668, they were all minors excepting Rowland. His will was probated in Lancaster 7 Sept., 1706, and it bears a wax seal with the above arms upon it. He left sons, Henry and Rowland. The arms are similar to those of Lawson of Brough Hall, Yorkshire, the latter being, "Argent a chevron between three martlets sable."

WHITING. Gloucester county.

Arms: On a chevron between three leopards' heads as many trefoils.

Crest: A wolf's head.

The above arms are on the tomb of Catharine Washington at Highgate, Gloucester county. She was the daughter of Col. Henry Whiting of said county, and the wife of Major John Washington. She died 7 Feb., 1743. The arms are presumably intended for Whiting and bear some resemblance to Whiting of the county of Sussex, who have in their arms "three leopards' faces."

TAYLOR. Norfolk county.

Arms: Argent, a saltire engrailed sable, cantoned with a heart in chief and base gules, and a cinquefoil in each flank vert.

Crest: A leopard holding in its dexter paw a cinquefoil.

Motto: Fide et fiducia.

Arms on the tomb of John Taylor in St. Paul's churchyard, Norfolk. He was born in the Parish of Fintree, Stirling, Scotland,

March, 1694, and died 25 Oct., 1744. He had one son, John, who married Sarah, daughter of Col. Robert Tucker and Joanna, his wife.. He had James Taylor, born 14 Dec., 1771, married his cousin, Sarah Newton, 11 June, 1800. He was Clerk of the Court and a prominent merchant, and died 7 June, 1826. He had a son, Tazewell Taylor, born in Norfolk 31st Jan., 1810, who had a son, Frederick S. Taylor, who was a member of the Virginia House of Delegates.

WYATT. Gloucester and New Kent counties.

Arms: Per fesse azure and gules, a horse barnacle argent, ringed or.

Crest: An ostrich ppr. holding in the beak a horseshoe argent.

The Virginia line descend from the ancient family of Wyatt in the county of Kent. The Rev. Hawte Wyatt came to Va. in 1621, with his brother Sir Francis Wyatt. He married twice and, according to a monument at Bexley, Kent, Eng., left issue in Virginia. Three of his sons were: Edward, George and John. Edward had a son, Conquest Wyatt, who patented land in Gloucester county in 1672. He was Vestryman of Petsworth in 1690, and Sheriff in 1705. George, son of the Rev. Hawte Wyatt, patented lands at Williamsburg in 1642. Henry Wyatt, son and heir of George, patented lands in Henrico county in 1679 and in 1686 was Vestryman of St. Peters, New Kent county. According to a deposition in Henrico Records, he was born in 1647.

SMITH. Lancaster county.

Arms: Sable a fesse dancettee between three lions rampant, each supporting a garb, all or.

Seal on a deed of Robert Smith and Elizabeth, his wife, of Lancaster county, dated 20 April, 1665. The arms correspond with those of Smith of Duffield, Derbyshire.

THOROUGHGOOD. Elizabeth City.

Arms: Sable on a chief argent, three buckles lozengy of the first.

Crest: A wolf's head argent, collared sable.

The pedigree of the Virginia family is contained in the Visitation of Essex (Harleian Society Pub.). They descended originally from John Thorogood of Chelston Temple, county Herts. Capt. Adam Thoroughgood, son of William of Norwich and Anne Edwards, his wife, was born in 1602 and came to Virginia in 1621. He was Commissioner and Burgess for Elizabeth City in 1629. In 1634 he removed to Lynnhaven Bay, in the present Princess Anne county, and was a member of the Council from there in 1637. He died in 1640. He married Sarah Offley of London (for her arms see Offley), and by her had issue: Adam, Ann, Sarah and Elizabeth. The son, Adam, was Lieut.-Col. and Burgess for Lower Norfolk in 1666 and Justice and Sheriff in 1669. He married a daughter of Col. Argall Yeardley of Northampton county, and had issue: Argall, John, Adam, Robert, Francis and Ann.

THORPE. York county.

Arms: Argent, a fesse nebulee between three trefoils slipped gules.

George Thorpe, buried 27 Sept., 1619, was a son· of Nicholas Thorpe of Manswell Court, Gloucestershire, by his first wife, Mary Wilkes, alias Mason, and niece of Sir John Mason, and grandson of Thomas Thorpe. In 1618 George Thorpe formed a partnership with Sir William Throckmorton, John Smith of Nibley and Richard Berkeley, to found a "New Berkeley in Virginia." He married, 1st, Margaret, daughter of Thomas Porter, who d.s.p., and 2ndly, Margaret, daughter of David Harris, by whom he had a son, William. There was a Richard Thorpe, who died in York county, Va., in 1660, who mentions sons, Richard and George, wife Elizabeth, and kinsman Major Otho Thorpe. These sons probably died unmarried, as the will of Richard Thorpe of Marston Parish, 12 March, 1669, gives all his estate to his stepfather, Otho Thorpe. The widow, Elizabeth Thorpe, married Otho Thorpe, baptized 16 Aug., 1606, at St. Martin, Middlesex, Eng. He was a Major and Justice of York county. He married three times, 1st, Elizabeth, widow of Richard Thorpe; 2nd, Dorothy, widow of Samuel Fenn, and 3rd, Frances, who survived him. Major Otho Thorpe died without issue in the Parish of All Hallows, London, devising his property to his nephew, Capt. Thomas Thorpe, who died 7 Oct., 1693, aged 48, as his tomb in Bruton Church, Williamburg, states. He left a son, Thomas Thorpe of King and Queen county.

WRAY. Elizabeth City county.

Arms: Azure on a chief or, three martlets gules.

Crest: An ostrich or.

Motto: El juste et vray.

The tomb of Capt. George Wray, in St. John's churchyard, Hampton, bears the above arms. He died 19 Apr., 1758 in the 61st year of his age, and was a member of an old family long settled in Elizabeth City. He married Helen Walker, and had issue: Jacob, a merchant at Hampton, whose will was dated 2 Feb., 1797; George, Keith, James, who was in Dunwiddle county in 1767, Ann, wife of John Stith, gent., of Stafford county.

SANDYS. James City.

Arms: Or, a fesse wavy between three crosses crosslet fitchee gules.

George Sandys, born 7 March, 1577, was the youngest son of Edwin Sandys, Archbishop of York. He was Treasurer of Virginia and member of the Council in 1621. He died at the house of his niece, the widow of Sir Francis Wyatt, and was buried at Bexley Abbey, Kent, 7 March, 1643.

PETTUS. James City county.

Arms: Gules a fess argent between three annulets or.

Crests: (1) A hammer erect argent, handle or. (2) Out of a ducal coronet or, a demi-lion argent, holding spear head gules, headed of the first.

Colonel Thomas Pettus is believed to have been the grandson of Sir John Pettus of Norwich, Norfolk. He patented land in James City county in 1643 and in 1645; in the latter year being a member of the Council. His first wife was Elizabeth, widow of Richard Durrent, and his second wife, Mourning ————, who afterwards married James Bray of the Council. The descendants of Col. Thomas Pettus have been distinguished in the history of their State.

SCARBOROUGH. Accomac county.

Arms: Or a chevron between three towers triple towered gules.

Crest: Out of a mural coronet gules a demi-lion or, holding upon the point of a lance of the first a Saracen's head ppr. wreathed azure.

Captain Edmund Scarborough was Justice of Accomac in 1631 and member of the House of Burgesses in 1629 and 1631-2. He married Hannah ——— and, dying in 1634-5, left issue: (1) Charles, afterward Sir Charles, born about 1616, entered Caius College, Cambridge, and was M. A. in 1639; he became physician to Charles II., James II. and William III., was a member of Parliament and was knighted 11 Aug., 1669. He died in 1693 and was buried at Cranford, Middlesex, leaving issue a son, Charles. (2) Colonel Edmund, son of Captain Edmund, was member of House of Burgesses for Northampton county, Speaker of the House in 1645; Justice, Sheriff and Surveyor-General of Virginia. He died 1670-1, and left by his wife, Mary: (1) Colonel Charles of Accomac, who died about 1703. The latter married more than once, one of his wives being a daughter of Gov. Richard Bennett. (2) Captain Edmund, Jr. (3) Littleton. (4) Matilda, married Colonel John West of Accomac. (5) Tabitha. The arms used by the Virginia branch are those of Scarborough of the county of Norfolk.

TOOKER. Prince George county.

Arms: Barry wavy of ten argent and azure on a chevron embattled and counter-embattled or, between three sea horses naiant of the first, five gouttes de poix.

Crest: A lion's gamb erased gules, charged with three billetts in pale or, and holding a battle axe or, headed azure.

Arms on the tomb of Henry Tooker at "Church Pastures," Prince George county. The inscription states that he was the eldest son of Henry Tooker of Winton in the county of Southampton, armiger, and that he died 20 Oct., 1710, aged 37 years. He married Dorothy, relict of John Tirrey, gent. The arms on the tomb are those of Tooker of Devonshire.

WITHERS. Frederick county.

Arms: Argent a chevron gules between three crescents sable.

Crest: A rhinoserous or.

Thomas and Elizabeth (Bonham) Withers had a son Reuben Withers, born 29 March, 1789. Thomas married a second time and removed to Kentucky, the son, Reuben, settling in Alexandria, Va., removing in 1816 to New York City. The latter's son Dunham Withers, was the father of A. W. Withers of Gloucester county, Va. In this branch of the family is an old armorial emblazoning, on the back of which is the following: "The arms of the family of Withers as granted to and confirmed to Sir Richard Withers of East Sheen, the ancestor of the poet, and registered in the Coll. of Arms, London."

WARREN. Charles City county.

Arms: Chequy or and azure on a canton gules a lion rampant argent.

Crest: Out of a ducal coronet or, a plume of five ostrich feathers argent, in front a griffin's claw or.

Motto: Tenebo.

The Virginia and Maryland Warrens descend from Sir Edward Warren, Knt., of Poynton, Cheshire, born 1563, died 1609, and who was descended from Earl Warren. Sir Edward, by his second wife, Anne, daughter of Sir William Davenport, had William, 5th child, who was in Virginia between 1633-40. Sir Edward's son and heir, John Warren of Poynton, died 1621, had a son, John, baptized 1606, who was living in St. Mary's county, Maryland, in 1642. He had, also, another son, Edward, born 1605, died 1667, whose third son, Col. Humphrey Warren, born 1632, was a planter in Charles county, Maryland, in 1666. His will was probated at Annapolis 25 Feb., 1694-5. The above Sir Edward Warren married thirdly, 1597, Susan, daughter of Sir William Booth of Dunham-Massey, and by her had Lieut. Radcliffe Warren, who was killed in Claiborne's raid on the Isle of Kent in 1635, and another son Thomas Warren, who patented 300 acres in Charles City county, Va., in 1635, 150 acres of which was in right of his wife, Susan Greenleaf, widow of Robert Greenleaf. Thomas Warren was Burgess in James City and Surry counties as late as 1666. He married, 2nd, in 1654, Elizabeth, widow of Major Robert Sheppard of Lower Chipoaks. He had sons, John, Richard and Thomas, but by which wife is not known.

CALVERT. Norfolk county.

Arms: Sable an inescutcheon within an orle of owls argent.

Crest: A horned owl argent.

Cornelius Calvert was a Justice of Norfolk in 1729 and member of the Common Council 7 July, 1741. He married, 29 July, 1719, Mary, daughter of the Rev. Jonathan Saunders and Mary Ewell, his wife. The will of Cornelius Calvert is dated 29 May, 1746, probated 18 June, 1747. He had issue: (1) Jonathan, born 23 Sept., 1720; (2) Maximilian, born 29 Oct., 1722; (3) Cornelius, born 13 March, 1725; (4) Thomas, born 8 Sept., 1726; (5) Saunders, born 31 Jan., 1728-9; (6) Joseph, born 14 April, 1732; (7) William, born 10 June, 1734; (8) Christopher, born 26 Sept., 1736; (9) John, born 19 Sept., 1739; (10) Mary, born 31 July, 1741; (11) Samuel,

born 8 Dec., 1743; (12) Elizabeth, born 27 Nov., 1745.
The arms used in Virginia by this family are the same as those
of Calvert of Lancaster, Eng.

NEVILLE. Elizabeth City county.

Tomb of John Neville at "Pembroke Farm," near Hampton.
The inscription states he was Vice-Admiral of the West Indies
fleet, and died on board the "Cambridge," 17 Aug., 1697, aged 53
years. The slab of the tomb is broken and defaced, the only part
of the arms to be distinguished being the crest, which is, a "demi-
lion rampant, holding a sword erect and issuing from a ducal
coronet."

WEBB. New Kent county.

Arms: Gules a cross between four falcons or.

Crest: Out of a ducal coronet or, a demi eagle rising gules.

The Williamsburg descendants of the Webb's of New Kent
possess some old silverware with the above arms engraved upon
it. Captain John Webb of New Kent, had: James, born 25 June,
1690; John, born 20 April, 1694; Jane, born 11 June, 1697; William,
born 11 Sept., 1699; Wentworth, born 5 May, 1702.

TIRREY: Prince George county.

Arms: Sable three chevronels between as many mullets argent.

Crest: A demi roebuck ppr. attired and unguled or, holding in
the mouth three ears of corn bladed of the first.

Arms on the tomb of John Tirrey, gent., at "Church Pastures,"
Prince George county, a part of the Brandon estate. The epitaph
states that he was born 4 Feb., 1649, in London, died 20 August,
1700. The arms on the slab, are those of Tirrey of London (confirmed 13 June, 1616), and impaled on the sinister side of the
shield are arms that are too worn to be decipherable. Alongside
is the tomb of Mrs. Dorothy Tooker, late relict of John Tirrey, gent.
She died 12 Dec., 1708.

ROSCOW. Warwick county.

Arms: A lion rampant.

Crest: A hand holding a dagger.

Arms on the tomb of William Roscow, gent., at Blunt Point,
Warwick county. He was born at Chorley in county of Lanca-
shire, 30 Nov., 1664, and died 2 Nov., 1700. The tomb of his wife
at the same place, states that she was Mary, daughter of Col.
William Wilson of Elizabeth City, and that she was born Oct.,
1675, and died 11 Jan., 1741. They had issue: (1) James of
Hampton, Receiver-General of Virginia 1761, d.s.p.; (2) William;
(3) Willis, born 1701, d.s.p. William Roscow, Jr., was Sheriff of
Warwick in 1729, Member of House of Burgesses 1726 and 1736.
He married Lucy, daughter of Col. William Bassett of "Eltham,"
New Kent county, and had issue, several sons who all d.s.p. before
1768. One son, James Roscow, was Justice of Warwick in 1769
and, it is believed, d.s.p. after 1774.

FITZHUGH. King George county.

Arms: Azure three chevrons brased in base interlaced or, a chief of the last.

Crest: On a cap of maintenance a wyvern, wings expanded argent.

Motto: Pro patria semper.

Colonel William Fitzhugh, the immigrant, was born in Bedford, Eng., being baptized 10 Jan., 1651, the son of Henry Fitzhugh. He came to Virginia and settled in Stafford county about 1670, calling his estate "Bedford." He was a Lieut.-Col. of Militia and member of the House of Burgesses. He married, 1 May, 1674, Sarah, daughter of John Tucker of Westmoreland county, and had issue: William, Henry, Thomas, George and John Fitzhugh. His eldest son, William, of "Eagles Nest," Stafford (now King George) county, died 1713-4. He was Clerk of Stafford and member of the House of Burgesses 1700-2, and member of the Council. He married Ann, daughter of Richard Lee of Westmoreland county, and she married, 2nd, Capt. Daniel McCarty of Westmoreland. By William Fitzhugh she had: (1) Henry; (2) Lettice, born 1707, died 1732, married. 1727, to George Turberville of Westmoreland; (3) Sarah, born 1710, died 1743, married, 1735, Edward Barradall, Attorney-General of Virginia. They are both buried in the same tomb in Bruton churchyard, Williamsburg, the slab bearing the Fitzhugh and Barradall arms impaled.

TURNER. King George county.

Arms: Ermine four fer de molines sable.

Crest: Argent a lion holding in the dexter paw a fer de moline sable.

Motto: Esse quam videri.

Arms on the tomb of Major Henry Turner, died 1757, at Smith's Mount, Westmoreland county. Major Turner was the son of Thomas and the grandson of Thomas Turner of King George. The latter was county clerk in 1723. His will is dated 19 Feb., 1757, probated 1758, his grandson, Major Henry Turner dying before him. Major Turner married Elizabeth, daughter of Col. Nicholas Smith. She died in 1752 and is buried in the same grave with her husband.

COLSTON. Richmond county.

Arms: Argent between two dolphins haurient respecting each other, an anchor, all ppr.

Crest: A dolphin embowed ppr.

Motto: Go thou and do likewise.

William Colston was a son of William Colston, Sheriff of Bristol, Eng., and came to Virginia about the middle of the seventeenth century. He had a son William, whose will dated 27 Oct., 1701, was probated on 3 Dec., 1701, in Richmond county. In it he mentions his sons, William and Charles, daughter, Susannah, son-in-law, Thomas Beale, and wife, Anne, decd. His wife, Anne, was a daughter of Major William Gooch of York county, who died in 1655, and she married ,first, Capt. Thomas Beale. William Colston, 3rd, had a daughter, Mary, who married John Smith, and a daughter, Frances, who married Joseph Morton of James City county. Charles Colston died in 1724, and married Rebecca, daughter of William Travers, and had a son, Travers Colston, born about 1712, who married, 1st, Alice Corbin Griffin, and, 2nd, Susan Opie Kennon.

ASTON.   Charles City county.

> Arms: Argent a fesse sable, in chief three lozenges of the last.
> Crest: A bull's head couped sable.
> Motto: Numini et patriae asto.

Lieut.-Col. Walter Aston represented Shirley Hundred Island 1629-30. He married twice, his widow, Hannah, marrying Col. Edward Hill. He was very probably descended from the Astons of Staffordshire. In the Visitation of London of 1634 is the following pedigree: "(1) Sir Walter Aston of Tixall, Co. Stafford, Knight; (2) Leonard Aston; (3) Walter Aston of Longdon, Stafford; (4) Walter Aston, third son of the last, now in the West Indies."

Lieut.-Col. Walter Aston had issue: (1) Susannah, relict in 1655 of Lieut.-Col. Edward Major; (2) Walter Aston, will dated 21 Dec., 1666, prob. 4 Feb., 1666-7; (3) Mary, married Richard Cocke, decd. ante 1666; (4) Elizabeth, married ———— Binns. Brown, in his "Genesis of the U. S.," says that Walter Aston, the immigrant, was cousin of Sir Walter Aston, Ambassador to Spain, 1620-25 and 1635-38, created a Baronet in 1611, and Lord Aston of Forfar, in the Scottish Peerage, 28 Nov., 1627. The tomb of Lieut.-Col. Walter Aston is at Westover. He died the 6th April, 1656, aged 49 years, and lived 28 years in this country. His son, Walter, died 29 Jan., 1666, aged 27 years and 7 months.

GRYMES.

> Arms: Or on three bars gules, as many martlets of the first; on a chief of the second two bars nebule argent.
> Crest: A martlet vert.

The above arms were granted to Richard Grymes of London by Robert Cook, 8 June, 1575. The following pedigree is taken from Nichol's "Topographica," Vol. III., pp. 155-7, and from the Parish Register of Camberwell, Surrey, and shows that there was another family named Grymes in Virginia in addition to the one settled in Middlesex county: (1) Richard Grymes of London; (2) Thomas Grymes of London, married Jane, daughter and co-heir of Thomas Muschamp of Peckham; (3) Sir Thomas Grymes of Peckham, Knt., 2 June, 1603; J. P. for Surrey; M. P. 1623; married Margaret, daughter of Sir George More of Loseley, Surrey; (4) Sir George Grymes, bapt. 10 Feb., 1604, knighted 9 Dec., 1628; buried 15 Oct., 1657; married Alice, daughter of Charles Lovell of West Harling, Norfolk; (5) Sir Thomas Grymes of Peckham, bapt. 10 May, 1638;

married Mary, daughter of Thomas Bond of Hogsdon, Middlesex. He sold his estate to his brother-in-law, Sir Thomas Bond, Bart. Sir Thomas Grymes had issue: (1) Edward, bapt. 6 Sept., 1660, buried 19 Apl., 1664; (2) Sir Thomas Grymes of Gloucester in 1694; (3) William in Virginia, having issue, a daughter; (4) Edmund in Ireland in 1694.

WALLACE. King George county.
Arms: Gules a lion rampant argent, within a bordure compony of the last and azure.
Crest: An ostrich holding in his beak a horseshoe ppr.
Motto: Libertas optima resumi.

Michael Wallace, M. D., of "Ellerslie," King George county, was born at Galrigs, Scotland, 11 May, 1719; died in Virginia, Jan —, 1767, will probated 4 June of that year. He married, 27 April, 1747, Elizabeth Brown, born 5 Oct., 1723, a daughter of Dr. Gustavus and Frances (Fowke) Brown of Charles county, Md.

Dr. Wallace had issue: (1) a daughter, born and died 1748; (2) William, born 1749, died 1750; (3) Gustavus Brown, born 1751, died 1802; (4) Michael, born 1753, married, 1775, Lettice (Smith) Wishart; (5) James, born 1755, died 1790; (6) William Brown, born 1757, married 1787, Barbara Fox; (7) Rebecca, d.s. an infant; (8) John, born 1761, died 1829, married 1792, Elizabeth Hooe; (9) Thomas, born 1761, twin brother of John, died 1818, married 1791, Mary Hooe.

Dr. Wallace was the son of William Wallace of Galrigs, who died ante 1734, whose father was Thomas Wallace of Cairnhill, and a direct descendant of Wallace of "Elderslie," Scotland. (See, "Wallace of Elderslie," Glasgow Arch. Soc. Trans., Vol. I., p. 102.)

SCOTT. Stafford county.
Arms: Or on a bend azure a star between two crescents; in a bordure argent eight stars.
Crest: A dove ppr.
Motto: Gaudia nuncio magna.

The Rev. Alexander Scott, M. A., of Overwharton Parish, Stafford county, was born at Dipple, Parish of Elgin, Scotland, the 20 July, 1686, and died at Dipple, Stafford county, 1 April, 1738. He married in Virginia, 20 May, 1717, Sarah (Gibbons) Brent, born in England 1692, died at Dipple, Va., 29 Oct., 1733. She was the daughter of William Gibbons of Wilts, Eng., gent., and widow of William Brent of Richlands, Stafford county, Va., and sister of Sir John Gibbons, M. P. for Middlesex.

The Rev. Alexander Scott was the eldest son of the Rev. John Scott, M. A., of Dipple, Scotland, born 1650, died 1726, and his wife, Helen Grant, died 7 Jan., 1769. Alexander and Sarah Scott had issue: (1) Helen, born 1737, married Cuthbert Bulitt; (2) Alexander, born 1740, d.s.p. ante 1762; (3) Catherine, born 1741, married William Brown, M. D.; (4) James, born 1742, died 1779, married ante 1762, Elizabeth Harrison; (5) Christian, born 4 March,

1745, married Col. Thomas Blackburn; (6) John, born 1747, died 1785, married, 1768, Elizabeth Gordon; (7) Robert, born 1749, died ante 1782, married Catherine Stone of Charles county, Md.

The above arms are engraved on the tomb of the Rev. Alexander Scott at Dipple, Stafford county.

CAMM. Williamsburg

Arms: Or a cross engrailed gules in the first quarter a crescent of the last.

Crest: A cross gules charged with a crescent or.

John Camm was the son of Thomas Camm of Hornsea, Yorkshire and was born in 1718. He took his B. A. at Trinity College, Cambridge, in 1741-2. In 1745 he became minister of Newport Parish, Isle of Wight county, Va., and in 1749 was Professor of Divinity in William and Mary College. He became President of the College in 1771. He died in 1779. He married in 1769, Elizabeth, daughter of Charles Hansford of York county. They had issue: (1) Anne, born 1770, died July 25, 1800, married Robert H. Waller, Clerk of York county, born 7 Jan., 1764; (2) Thomas (Rev.), married Elizabeth, daughter of Thomas Pescud. Thomas Camm was rector of Charles Parish, York county from 1794 to 1798 and subsequently of Denbigh Parish, Warwick county; (3) Robert, drowned when young; (4) John, born 2 Dec., 1775, studied law and removed after 1794 to Amherst county, and was Clerk of the Court there from 1814 to 1818. He married Elizabeth, daughter of Thomas Powell; (5) Elizabeth Camm, married Anthony Whitaker.

President John Camm used a book plate upon which was engraved the above arms.

CONWAY. Northampton and Lancaster counties.

Arms: Sable on a bend argent cotised ermine, a rose gules, between two annulets of the last.

Crest: A Moor's head side faced ppr, banded round the temples argent and azure.

Motto: Fide et amore.

Edwin Conway of the county of Worcester, England, came to Virginia in 1640, and in 1642 was Clerk of Northampton county. He was born about 1610, and died in Lancaster county in 1675. He married, 1st, in England, Martha, daughter of Richard Eltonhead, Esq., of Lancashire. He moved from Northampton to Lancaster county about 1652; his second wife being either a sister or sister-in-law of John Carter of Corotoman. His known issue, gathered from deeds in Lancaster Court House: (1) Edwin, born about 1640-4, died 1698, married, 1st, Sarah Fleete; married, 2nd, in 1695, Elizabeth Thompson; (2) Eltonhead (daughter), born about 1646, married about 1662 Henry Thacker.

Edwin Conway, second of the name, by his first wife, Sarah Fleete, daughter of Lieut.-Col. Henry Fleete of Lancaster county, had: (1) Edwin, born 1681, died 1763, married, 1st, in 1704, Ann

Ball, and, 2nd, Ann Hack; (2) Mary, born about 1686, died 1730, married, 1st, in 1703, John Daingerfield, and, 2nd, in 1707, Major James Ball.

Edwin Conway, by his second marriage to Elizabeth Thompson, had Francis, born 1697, married, 1720, to Rebecca Catlett.

There are several deeds at Lancaster Court House made by Edwin Conway, 3rd of the name, bearing the above arms.

DALE. Lancaster county.

Arms: Gules on a mount vert a swan argent, membered and ducally gorged or.

Crest: On a chapeau gules turned up ermine, a heron argent, beaked, legged and ducally gorged or.

Edward Dale, gent., was a brother-in-law of Sir Grey Skipwith, 3rd, Baronet of Prestwould, Leicestershire, both of whom settled in Lancaster county, Virginia. Edward Dale was appointed Clerk in 1655, holding this office until 10 May, 1674. He was Justice from 1669 to 1684; Sheriff in 1670, '71, '79 and 1680, and member of the House of Burgesses in 1677 and 1682.

In the Lancaster records there is a letter from Sir Grey Skipwith, which shows that Edward Dale's wife was the former's sister, Diana Skipwith, daughter of Sir Henry Skipwith of Prestwould, Leicestershire. In the several records of the county he is frequently referred to as Edward Dale, "Gent.," or "Major" Edward Dale. His will was recorded in March, 1695, but the original cannot be found. He left two daughters: (1) Catharine, who married Thomas Carter of Lancaster; (2) Elizabeth, who married William Rogers of Northumberland.

In the existing Dale records of Lancaster no armorial seal can be found attached. His son-in-law, Thomas Carter, who married his daughter Catharine, used a seal bearing the above crest, which has until now been ascribed as a crest of the Carter family. It is undoubtedly, however, the crest and armorial bearing of Edward Dale, and is the same as Dale of London and Northampton, from which family he probably was descended. This seal is attached to Carter deeds as late as 1776 and it has descended in the family from the distaff side of the house. (See Capt. Thomas Carter of Lancaster county.)

MALLORY. New Kent and Elizabeth City counties.

Arms: Or, a lion rampant gules collared argent.

Crest: A nag's head couped gules.

The Virginia Mallorys descend from the ancient family of that name of Studley Royal, Yorkshire. The manor of Studley Royal came into the family through the marriage of William Mallory of Hutton Conyers (whose will, proved 24 April, 1475, is preserved at York) with Dionisia, co-heiress with her sister Isabel, and daughter of William Tempest of Studley, who died 4 Jan., 1444. William Mallory was the representative of an ancient family who possessed Hutton Conyers, Yorkshire, by the marriage of Sir

Christopher Mallory (son of Sir Thomas and a daughter of Lord Zouch) with Joan, daughter and heiress of Robert Conyers, whose ancestor, Robert Conyers, possessed it in 1246.

A very full account of the Mallorys of Studley can be found in Walbran's, "Memoir of the Lords of Studley in Yorkshire."

Coming to a more recent date, we find Sir William Mallory of Studley and Hutton, heir to his brother Christopher. He was High Sheriff of Ripon, and M. P. for Yorkshire in 1585. He married Ursula, daughter of George Gayle, Esq., of York, Master of the Mint there, and sometime Lord Mayor. Sir William's will was probated 5 April, 1603.

Thomas Mallory, son of the above, was Dean of Chester. He married Elizabeth, daughter of Richard Vaughan, Bishop of Chester, and died 3 April, 1644. He left issue: (1) Richard; (2) William, knighted in 1642, d.s.p.; (3) Thomas, of whom later; (4) George; (5) John; (6) Avery; (7) Everard; (8) Philip; (9) Francis; (10) Jane; (11) Katherine (Martha?); (12) Elizabeth; (13) Mary.

Philip Mallory, son of the Dean, was born 1617; matriculated 28 May, 1634, at Corpus Christi, Oxford; B. A. 1637; M. A. 1639. He was in Virginia as early as 1656 and was minister in York county in 1660. His wife was Catherine, daughter of Robert Batte, Vice-Master of University Coll., Oxford. Rev. Philip Mallory returned to England, and his will was proved in London 27 July, 1661. He left all his plantations in Virginia to his nephew, Roger Mallory.

Thomas Mallory, son of the Dean, and brother of Philip, was baptized at Davenham, 27 Aug., 1605; matriculated at New Coll., Oxford, 15 Oct., 1624; B. A. 7 May, 1628; M. A. 17 Jan., 1631-2. He became Rector of Easington, Oxfordshire, 1632, and in 1634 was presented to the family living of Northenden, Cheshire. On the 30th of July, 1660, he was made Canon of Chester, and died at Brindle, near Eccleston in Lancashire, in 1671. He was twice married, his first wife being Jane, who died 12 Feb., 1638, his second wife being Frances. In his will he mentions "sonne Roger in Virginia, sonne Thomas in Virginia." Many particulars of the Dean and his son, Thomas, can be found in the "Cheshire Sheaf"; also of Thomas in the "Dictionary of National Biography."

Roger Mallory patented land in Virginia in 1660 and he was also the heir of his uncle, the Rev. Philip Mallory. He settled in that part of New Kent county which later became King and Queen, and, still later, King William county. He was a Justice of New Kent in 1680 and of King and Queen county in 1693, having also the title of Captain. In 1704-5 he was a Justice of King William county.

William Mallory, son of Roger, settled in Elizabeth City county as early as 1680. He married Ann, daughter of Thomas Wythe, gent., Justice of that county. His will was probated 15 Feb., 1720, in which he mentions sons, Francis and William, and daughters, Mary and Ann.

Francis, son of William Mallory, married Ann, widow of Edward Myhill. His will was probated in Elizabeth City 18 July, 1744. His only son, Johnson Mallory, married Diana (King?). His will probated 5 May, 1762, mentions daughters, Margaret, Mary and Ann King and sons, Francis and Edward. Francis, son of Johnson Mallory, was married twice before he was twenty-one, and once just afterward, his last wife being Mary, sister of Miles King, of Norfolk. He was a Lieut.-Col. of the Elizabeth City Militia, June, 1776, and was killed in action 8 March, 1781. He left daughters, Diana, Elizabeth and Mary, and a son, Charles King Mallory. The latter was born about 1781. He was a member of the Virginia Legislature and the Council, and Lieutenant-Governor of Virginia during the War of 1812. He married Frances Lowry Stevenson, a daughter of Lieut. William Stevenson of the Revolution, and left issue: Francis Mallory, M. C.; William S. Mallory; Colonel Charles K. Mallory of the Confederate Army; Catherine Beverley Mallory and Mary King Mallory. Among living descendants of the foregoing are: Professor Francis Mallory of the Virginia Military Institute (grandson of Francis); William S. Mallory of Charlotte, N. C. (son of William); Lieut. Charles K. Mallory, U. S. N., retired (grandson of Charles); and Lieut.-Col. John S. Mallory, U. S. A. (son of Charles), who married Sarah, daughter of the late J. H. Reed of Portland, Oregon, and who has issue, Henry Reed Mallory, born 1892, and John Stevenson Mallory, born 1894.

ARCHER. Henrico county.

Arms: Azure three arrows argent.

Crest: Out of a mural coronet gules a dragon's head argent.

Motto: Fortitudo.

The first of this family in Virginia was George Archer, who, in 1665, had a grant of 550 acres of land on Tunstalls Creek, Henrico county; he also was granted other patents. He died in 1677, in that part of Henrico which is now Chesterfield county. It is not known whom he married, but he left issue: (1) George, born 1654, died 1731, a vestryman of Bristol Parish in 1721, who married Elizabeth, sister of William Harris of Henrico; (2) Elizabeth, married Thomas Branch of Henrico; (3) John of Henrico, vestryman and Justice in 1713, married, 1st, Frances, relict of Thomas Shippey; married, 2nd, Martha, daughter of Major Peter Field of Henrico; (4) Margaret.

The arms are from the book plate of Col. William Archer of Amelia county, who was a Justice in 1743. He was a grandson of John and Martha (Field) Archer of Henrico.

BERNARD. Nansemond county.

Arms: Argent a bear rampant sable, muzzled or.

Col. William Bernard settled in Nansemond county about 1640. He was a member of the Council 1642-3 and in 1659-60. He married about 1655, Lucy, widow of Major Lewis Burwell and daughter of Robert Higginson, and in that year had a son, George.

Col. Bernard died 31 March, 1665, his relict afterward marrying Col. Philip Ludwell.

Col. William Bernard was a brother of Sir Robert Bernard, Bart., of Brampton Hall, Huntingdonshire. The Baronetcy was created in 1662 and became extinct in 1789, Sir Robert's will is dated 5 Dec., 1665, and probated 15 May, 1666, in it he says: "I give to my brother William's son, now at Brampton, 100 pounds if he lives to be eighteen, and I leave him to my son John to bring up, and some care to be had to inquire what his father left him in Virginia." In addition to the son George, Col. Bernard is said to have had two daughters, Lucy and Elizabeth.

BECKWITH. Richmond county.

Arms: Argent a chevron between three hind's heads erased gules.

Crest: An antelope ppr. in the mouth a branch vert.

Motto: Joir en bien.

Sir Marmaduke Beckwith, Baronet, of Aldborough, Yorkshire, was born there in 1687. He was the son of Sir Roger Beckwith and Elizabeth Jennings. Elizabeth was the daughter of Sir Edmund Jennings, Knt., of Ripon and his wife Margaret, daughter of Sir Edward Barkham, Knt. and Bart., of Middlesex.

Sir Marmaduke settled in Richmond county, of which he was clerk and died at an advanced age. His known children were: (1) Jonathan, married Rebecca Barnes; (2) Tarpley, born 2 Oct., 1718, died 7 Nov., 1728; (3) Elizabeth, born 15 Oct., 1723, died 7 April, 1726; (4) Margaret, born 27 July, 1725; (5) Mary, born 12 June, 1727; (6) Rebecca, married Major John Bellfield; (7) Marmaduke, married Sybil, daughter of Major Elsie. One of the daughters, either Mary or Margaret, married Joseph Morton of James City, gent. This is proved from a deed dated 20 Dec., 1756, from Sir Marmaduke Beckwith of Richmond county to his son-in-law, Joseph Morton.

HENDERSON. Augusta county.

Arms: Gules three piles issuing out of the sinister side argent, on a chief of the last a crescent azure between two ermine spots.

Crest: A cubit arm ppr. the hand holding a star or, ensigned with a crescent azure.

Motto: Sola virtus nobilitat.

John, James and Samuel Henderson, sons of William and Margaret Henderson, came to Virginia about 1740, and settled in Augusta county, where they still have descendants. In an old Bible belonging to Lieut. James Henderson of the French and Indian Wars, are the following entries: "This record set down from the memory of James Henderson, now aged 75."

"William Henderson, gent., and Margaret Bruce married 7 Feb., 1705. John, son to William, born 9 Feb., 1706; James, son to William, born 17 Jan., 1708; Bruce, son to William, born 10 May, 1710, died Sept., 1719; Samuel, son to William, born 28 Nov., 1713.

Grandsons to John Henderson, gent., Fifeshire, Scotland. William Henderson, born 30 April, 1676, died 1 Aug., 1757; Margaret Henderson, born 1 March, 1680-1, died 15 Dec., 1759; Jean Henderson Stuart, died in child bed, March, 1730, aged 19; John Henderson died 1 May, 1766, aged 60; Samuel Henderson, died 19 Jan., 1782." Then follows the record of marriage of James Henderson to Martha Hamilton, daughter of Audley Hamilton and Elenor, his wife, 23 June, 1738. Their children were: David, William, John, James, Sarah, Joseph, Jean, Samuel, Archibald and Margaret.

James Henderson, born 1708, died 1784, was a Lieutenant in the Augusta County Militia, and in 1758 received pay for services in the French and Indian Wars. (Crozier's "Va. Colonial Militia," p. 60.) His son, John Henderson, born 1740, died 1787, married in 1765, Anne Givens, youngest sister of the wife of General Andrew Lewis. In 1774 he served in the Battle of Point Pleasant as a lieutenant in Capt. John Lewis' company from Botetourt county. He removed to Greenbrier, and in 1775 and 1776 was a Captain in the Militia of that county. On 6 Dec., 1776, he enlisted as a Corporal in Capt. Gregory's company, Gen. Daniel Morgan's Virginia Regiment, and served until Nov. 1779. He was a Justice of Greenbrier in 1780. He left at his death in 1787, four sons and two daughters: (1) Samuel Henderson, married Sarah Donnally in 1794, a daughter of Col. Andrew Donnally. He settled on a grant of land his father had received for military services, and which was situated on the Great Kanawha River. Here, in 1811, he built the second brick house in Mason county. He died in 1838, leaving issue, John Givens, who lived at the home plantation, and Charles and Andrew Henderson, both lawyers who d.s.p. (2) Col. John Henderson, born 1768, died 1824, was the most prominent of the sons of Lieut. John Henderson. He was Commissioner of Revenue for Greenbrier in 1786 and 97. In the latter year he moved with his family to the Henderson grant, in what later became Mason county. Here, in 1804, he was Justice of the First Court, Sheriff in 1815 and 1818, Member of the Va. Legislature in 1809, 1810, 1811, 1812, 1813, 1814, 1817, 1818, 1819 and 1820. He was also Colonel of the Mason County Militia for many years, some of his old regimental orders showing that he served in the War of 1812. In 1792 he married Elizabeth Stodghill, daughter of John and Elizabeth Harvey Stodghill, by whom he had six daughters. (3) Margaret Henderson, daughter of Lieut. John Henderson, born 1771, died 1853, married in 1795, William Vawter, and left many descendants who became prominent in Va. and W. Va. One son and four of her grandsons being captains in the Confederate army.

The Henderson family is of Scotch ancestry, the above arms being engraved on the watch used by Lieut. John Henderson, who died in 1787. The arms are also found in wax on a paper signed by Col. John, who died in 1824. The watch and paper are now owned by a great-great-grandson, Dr. Joseph Lyon Miller, Thomas, W. Va.

BEVERLEY. Middlesex county.

Arms: Ermine, a rose gules, barbed and seeded ppr.

Robert Beverley, the immigrant, came from Yorkshire (Burke's "Landed Gentry") to Virginia in 1663 and settled in Middlesex county, of which he was a Justice in 1673, and Clerk of the House of Burgesses in 1670. His first wife was Mary, said to have been a daughter of George Keeble of Lancaster county, and his second, Catherine, either the daughter of Major Theophilus Hone of James City county or his widow, it is uncertain which, whom he married in Gloucester county, 28 March, 1679 (Christ Church Par. Reg.). Major Beverley died 15 March, 1686. He had issue by his first wife: Peter, Robert and Harry Beverley, and a daughter, Mary, who married in 1694 William Jones of King and Queen. By his second wife, Catherine Hone, he had issue: William, bapt. 4 Jan., 1680, married Judith, daughter of Christopher Wormeley, and widow of Corbin Griffin, and died 1702. John, in 1687 under the guardianship of his brother Peter, he d.s.p. Thomas, d.s.p. 1686. Christopher, bapt. 19 Feb., 1686, he was Sheriff of King and Queen in 1729 and d.s.p. Catharine Beverley, married John Robinson, son of Christopher Robinson, Secretary of State and member of the Council, and nephew of John Robinson, Bishop of London.

Col. Peter Beverley, eldest son of Major Robert, the immigrant, was clerk of Gloucester county, and also of the House of Burgesses 1691-99; he was also Speaker of the House 1700-14, Treasurer of Virginia 1710-23, member of the Council in 1719, and died in 1728. He married Elizabeth, daughter of Major Robert Peyton of "Isleham," Gloucester county, and left issue, two daughters, Susanna and Elizabeth.

Robert Beverley, second son of Major Robert, lived in King and Queen county, of which he was clerk 1699-1702, member of the House of Burgesses for Jamestown 1699, 1700, 1702, 1706, etc. He was clerk of the Council in 1697. He married Ursula, died 31 Oct., 1698, aged 16 years and 11 months, daughter of Col. William Byrd, leaving a son William.

Captain Harry Beverley, third son of Major Robert, was Justice of Middlesex in 1700. He removed to Spotsylvania county about 1720, and was for a number of years presiding Justice. He died 1730, and married about 1700, Elizabeth, daughter and heiress of Robert Smith of "Brandon," Middlesex, by whom he had issue: Elizabeth, Robert, Susanna, Mary, Catherine, Judith, Peter, Agatha, Anne and Margaret.

There has been some confusion in regard to the correct arms of the Beverley family. Upon the will of the first Major Robert Beverley, preserved at Middlesex Court House, there is a wax seal, which has upon it, "Quarterly argent and gules, a rose counterchanged, barbed vert." William Beverley of "Blandfield," son of Robert Beverley, 2nd, and grandson of the immigrant, writing to his London agent in 1739, states, "That he sends him a seal which he wishes recut, that it was made in 1723, but had the wrong arms engraved upon it, that the arms his father used were, ' red rose seeded and barbed in a field ermine, with a unicorn's head for crest, and not the three bull's heads.' " On a bond of William Beverley, 1736, in Essex County Court, there is a wax seal with the following arms, "Argent a chevron sable, on a chief of the second three bulls' heads cabossed of the first." These are the arms spoken of by William Beverley in his letter, and were, according to him, incorrect. The old tomb of Ursula (Byrd) Beverley, who died in 1698 bore Beverley and Byrd impaled, for the former, "Ermine a rose gules, barbed and seeded ppr." The Beverley book plates bear the arms of the three bulls' heads and chevron, but it is evident that they are incorrect, and that the proper arms are as given above.

CLARKE. York county.

Arms: Quarterly. (1) Or on a bend engrailed azure, a cinquefoil of the field. (2) Argent on a chevron gules, between three Columbines azure, as many crescents or. (3) Azure a cross between five billets saltire argent in each quarter. (4) Or on a cross sable five crescents argent.

John Clarke of York county was decd. ante 1645. (York county records.) There is a power of atty. at Yorktown, dated 29 Dec., 1671, which recites, "That John Clarke of Wrotham in the county of Kent, Esq., nephew and sole heir-at-law of John Clarke, formerly of Virginia, merchant, decd., who was a son of Sir John Clarke, Knt., of Wrotham, long since deceased, and younger and only brother of Sir William Clarke, Knt. (lately decd.), which said Sir William Clarke was father of me, John Clarke, his son and heir."

In the Visitation of Kent there is a pedigree of the family which shows that John Clarke of Virginia was born in 1614, and that he had an elder brother, William, born in 1610, and a sister Cecilia. He was son of Sir John Clarke and Elizabeth, daughter of Sir William Steed of Hautsham.

BRODNAX. York county,

Arms: Or two chevrons gules, on a chief of the second three cinquefoils argent.

Crest: Out of a mural crown argent, a griffin's head or, winged and collared gules, charged with three cinquefoils argent.

The above arms were granted by Clarenceux King of Arms, William Camden, to Thomas Brodnax, gent., of Godmersham of the county of Kent. The family was of some antiquity in England, the name appearing in Kent as early as the time of Henry IV. Berry, in his "Kentish Genealogies" gives the pedigree of the family from the time of Robert Brodnax, who married Alice Scappe, died 1487, down to the year 1794, when the direct line of descent in England became extinct. Sir William Brodnax, 8th in descent from Robert, was knighted by Charles II. in 1664. In 1727 Thomas Brodnax assumed the name of May in pursuance of the will of Sir Thomas May, from whom he derived a considerable estate in Sussex and London. Still later he exchanged the name of May for Knight, upon his inheritance of landed estate in Hampshire. Thomas, a son of the above, married Catherine, the daughter of Dr. Wadham Knatchbull, Chancellor of Durham and Dean of Canterbury. He d.s.p. 23 Oct., 1794, leaving his property to his cousin, Edward Austin, a brother of Jane Austin, the novelist, who also changed his name to that of Knight. Godmersham Park, the seat for many generations of the Brodnax family, at the death of Thomas Knight, passed into the hands of the Austin-Knight family, the present owner being Montague Knight, Esq.

The first of the family to come to Virginia was Major John Brodnax, who settled in York county. His will is dated 23 July, 1657, and was probated 16 Nov. of that year. In it he mentions, "His wife Dorothy, daughter Elizabeth, youngest sons, William and Robert; eldest son, Thomas, to be executor, living at 'the Golden Griffin' with Mr. Thomas Turges in Fenchurch street; son John, living with Mr. Joseph King in 'ye Golden Sun' in Gratious street."

Major John Brodnax was the uncle of Sir William Brodnax (Berry's Kent). He was born at Godmersham, and his title of "Major" evidently indicates that he was a Cavalier officer, as his name does not appear in the Militia lists of the Colony. The character of his personal estate would also indicate the same, as it included three periwigs, a rapier and belt, five broadcloth suits, slippers, ribbons, cuffs, etc. Towards the end of the 17th century two brothers, John and William Brodnax, came to Virginia. They were the sons of Robert Brodnax, goldsmith, of London, and grandsons of Major John Brodnax. They were born at Godmersham, and John being the oldest preceeded his brother in Virginia by some few years. William Brodnax was born 28 Feb., 1675, and married Rebecca Travis of Jamestown. He died in 1727 and was buried at James City Island. He brought with him a large emblazoning of the family arms, also the portraits of his father, Robert, and mother, Ann Brodnax, painted by Sir Peter Lely; a seal with his arms engraved upon it, and his father's Bible, in which is recorded his own date of birth. He was a member of the House of Burgesses from James City in 1718, 1720, 1722, 1723 and 1726. He left issue, and from William descend the branch now in North Carolina.

John Brodnax, brother of William, settled first in Henrico county where he had several large land grants. He married Mary, the daughter of William and Mary Skerme of Henrico. He afterwards removed to Williamsburg, where he engaged in the business of a goldsmith, and where he died in 1719, leaving his brother William and his oldest son, Robert, administrators of his estate. His children were: Robert, William, Winfield, Mary Ann and Sarah. But few of the name of Brodnax are now left in Virginia, one of the direct descendants being Dr. John W. Brodnax of Manchester, Va.

CHICHESTER. Lancaster county.

Arms: Chequy or and gules, a chief vair.

Crest: A heron with wings expanded, holding in the beak a snake all ppr.

Motto: Ferme en foy.

The Virginia branch of this family descends from the ancient house of Chichester of the county of Devon. (1) Sir Roger Chichester, knighted at Calais, died 1370. (2) John, son of Sir Roger, born 1365, died 1384, married Thomasine Raleigh, daughter of Sir John Raleigh, granddaughter of Sir Robert de Raleigh and wife Laura Peverel (daughter of Sir Hugh Peveral), great-granddaughter of Sir Walter de Raleigh and wife, Lady Sabilla de Umfraville (daughter of Gilbert de Umfraville and his wife, Matilda, Countess of Angus), and great-great-granddaughter of Sir Peter de Raleigh, Lord of Raleigh, who died 1223, and whose wife was Matilda de Braybroc, daughter of Galfridus de Braybroc, Lord of Braybroc. (3) John, son of John above, born 1386, died 14 Dec., 1437, married, 1424, Alice, daughter of John Walton and his wife Johanna de Dinham (daughter of Robert de Dinham and his wife, Emma Moels, who was the daughter of Roger Moels and his wife, Alice le Prouse, the latter being the daughter of William le Prouse, Lord of Orton). (4) Richard, son of John Chichester, born 23 Feb., 1424, married Margaret Kaynes of Winkley, daughter of Nicholas Kaynes. (5) Nicholas, son of Richard Chichester, born 1452, married Christine Paulett, daughter of Sir William Paulett. (6) John, son of Nicholas Chichester, married Johanna Brett. He died 22 Feb., 1537. (7) John, son of John Chichester of Raleigh and wife Joan Brett, inherited from his father the Manor of Widworthy. He married 6 Nov., 1538, Katherine, daughter of Thomas Peard of Taustock, Devon. (8) John, eldest son of John Chichester, buried at Widworthy, 19 Feb., 1609, will proved same year; married Dorothy, daughter of Hugh Daubeney of Waxford, Somerset. (9) Hugh of Widworthy, eldest son of John Chichester, was baptized at Widworthy 7 June, 1573, buried 22 Feb., 1641, married Martha, daughter of Richard, Duke of Otterton, Devon. (10) Richard, eldest son and heir of Hugh Chichester, baptized at Widworthy, 13 June, 1600, died in his father's life time, was buried at Widworthy, 17 March, 1638; married Joan, daughter of John Smithes of Kington, Somerset; married at Kington 22 May, 1625; buried at Widworthy 5 August, 1643. (11) John, heir to his grandfather Hugh Chichester, was baptized at Widworthy, 11 Oct., 1626, buried 11 June, 1661, will dated 3 June, 1661; married Margaret, daughter of John Ware of Hallerton and Silverton, Devon, and his wife, Margaret, daughter of Thomas Dart of Silverton. (12) Richard, second son of John Chichester of Widworthy and Margaret Ware, was born at Silverton 5 March, baptized 16 March, 1657. He married, 1st, in England, Anna ————, came to Virginia in 1702, bringing with him his son John, and settled in Lancaster county. He married, 2nd, 11 July, 1719, Ann Chinn, widow of William Fox (Lancaster county M. L. Bonds, p. 48, Crozier's Va. Marriages).

Richard Chichester's will is dated 14 April, 1734. (13) John, son of Richard Chichester and Anna ————, was baptized at Widworthy 10 May, 1681, and died in Virginia, Oct. —, 1728; married Elizabeth Symes of Dorset, England, who was buried at Powerstock, Dorset, Jan., 1728. (14) Richard, son of John Chichester and Elizabeth Symes, died in England, 30 Dec., 1743, and was buried at Powerstock 3 January. He married, 3 July, 1734 (Lancaster county M. L. Bonds, p. 49, Crozier's Va. Marriages), Ellen Ball, daughter of Col. William Ball and Hannah Beale, and lived at "Fairweathers," Lancaster county, Virginia. (15) Richard, son of Richard Chichester and Ellen Ball, married, 1st, 7 June, 1759 (Lancaster County M. L. Bonds, p. 52, Crozier's Va. Marriages), by this marriage there was no issue. He married, 2nd, Sarah McCarty, daughter of Col. Daniel McCarty and Sarah Ball. They lived at "Newington," Fairfax county, and were buried there. (16) Richard McCarty Chichester, son of Richard Chichester of Newington and Sarah McCarty, was born 1769 and died 1793. He married Ann Thomson Mason, daughter of Thomas Mason of Stafford (brother of George Mason of Gunston), and Elizabeth Barnes. After his death his widow returned to her home in Loudoun county, and died there in 1817. Ann Mason Chichester, daughter of the above, was born 16 Oct., 1789, and died 12 July, 1882. She married Charles Pendleton Tutt, and lived at "Locust Hill," Loudoun county. (17) George Mason Chichester, son of Richard McCarty Chichester, born 2 March, 1793, died 12 Dec., 1835; married 23 Dec., 1824, Mary Bowie, daughter of Washington Bowie and Margaret John, of Georgetown, D. C., and lived at "Ivon," Loudoun county. The present owner of "Ivon" is Arthur Mason Chichester, Esq.

CHICHELEY. Lancaster county.

Arms: Or a chevron between three cinquefoils gules.

Crest: A tiger passant argent, holding in the mouth a man's leg couped at the thighs ppr., the foot downward.

Sir Henry Chicheley, son of Sir Henry Chicheley, Bart., of Wimpole, Cambridgeshire, served in the Royal Army during the Civil War, and came to Virginia in 1649. He was Burgess for Lancaster county, 1656, member of the Council 1670, Deputy-Governer 28 Feb., 1673-4, acting Governor Dec., 1678 to 16 May, 1680. He married Agatha Eltonhead, the widow of Ralph Wormeley of "Rosegill," Middlesex county, and died 5 Feb., 1682.

FEILDING. King and Queen county.

Arms: Argent on a fess azure, three lozenges or.

This family had but two generations in Virginia bearing the name, viz.: Henry Feilding, gent., and his daughter Frances. The arms described above are on a wax seal attached to the will of Henry Feilding, who died in King and Queen county in 1712, bequeathing the bulk of his estate to his daughter Frances, who married John Lewis of Warner Hall, Gloucester county. From this marriage have descended some of the most prominent and cultured people of the South. One of their sons was Colonel Feild-ing Lewis, who married Betty Washington, the only sister of General George Washington. Old silver plate still in possession of the family show the above arms engraved upon it, which are those of the Earls of Denbigh.

CREYKE...

Arms: Per fess argent and sable, on a pale three martlets. In "Familiae Minorum Gentium," Vol. III., p. 952 there is given the descent of a Henry Creyke, who was in Virginia. The pedi-gree begins with Alexander Creyke of Kylne and Colleston, living in 1413, from whom descend Gregory Creyke, married 9 Sept. 1623, Ursula, daughter of John Legard. Gregory and Ursula had with other children, Henry Creyke, born 16 July, 1637, Captain of a merchant ship, and who died in Virginia. John Creyke, born 6 Jan., 1626, and who died in the West Indies.

SMITH. Essex county.

Arms: Argent a fess dancette between three roses gules barbed vert.

Wax seal on the will of Colonel Joseph Smith, 1728, at Tappa-hannock, Essex. The arms are similar to Smyth of Honyngton, Lincolnshire.

BUTLER. Westmoreland county.

A silver waiter, at one time belonging to the Butler family, and now in the possession of Mr. Laurence Washington, has engraved upon it the arms of Butler and Beckwith quarterly. 1st and 4th for Beckwith, "a chevron between three hinds' heads." 2nd and 3rd for Butler, "a chief indented and a saltire with three covered cups." Crest: Out of a plume of ostrich feathers, a fal-con rising, for Butler.

The Butlers were a Westmoreland county family. Jane Butler, daughter of Caleb Butler, marrying Augustine Washington.

RODES. Louisa county

Arms: Argent a lion passant guardant gules, between two acorns azure, within two bendlets ermines.

Crest: An arm couped at the elbow argent, holding an oak branch or fructed azure.

In "Familiae Minorum Gentium," Vol. II., pp. 583-87, Harleian Society Publications, the following pedigree is given: John Rodes, fifth son of Sir Francis Rodes and Elizabeth (Lascelles) Rodes, married Elizabeth, daughter of Simon Jason of Edial, Staf-fordshire, and had issue: (1) John, living in 1695; (2) Francis, resided in Maryland, where he was twice married, but is now (1698) in England, and has issue; (3) Charles, third son, living in Virginia, where he is lately married, 1695; (4) Anne.

It is believed that John Rodes, who was born in Virginia, 6 Nov., 1697, died 3 May, 1775, was a son of the above-named Charles Rodes. He was a vestryman of Fredericksville Parish,

Louisa county in 1765. In Oct., 1766, John Rodes and Mary, his wife, made a deed of gift to their son, Clifton Rodes of Louisa. They had four sons, Clifton, Charles, John and David. The name of Clifton is found in the English branch of the Rodes family, and on account of its peculiarity as a given name, is a strong indication that the American branch was of the same line as Sir Francis Rodes.

TAZEWELL. Brunswick county.

Arms: Vaire purpure and ermine, on a chief gules a lion passant or.

Crest: A demi-lion purpure, in the paws a chaplet of eight roses gules.

In the Visitation of London made in 1664, is a pedigree of the Tazewell family. They were originally of the county of Somerset. James, son of William Tazewell of "Buckland Newton," was bapt. at the parish church July, 1588, county of Dorset. His first wife was Mary, daughter of ———— Hunt of Forston, Dorset, and died in 1659. He died in 1663. His son, James Tazewell, was a merchant in London, and married, 1st, 26 March, 1649, Elizabeth Upsal, who died in 1667. He married. 2nd, in 1673, Elizabeth, daughter of John Kingsmill of Andover; she died 1702, s.p. James Tazewell died 26 March, 1683. In 1663 James Tazewell was seised of the manor of South Brent, Somerset, and in 1672 owned the manor of Limington, Somerset. James Tazewell, eldest son and heir, born 20 Feb., 1650, succeeded his father in the manor of Limington. He married Ann Kingsmill, and had issue, three sons and three daughters. The third son, William Tazewell, baptized 17 July, 1690, went to Virginia in 1715, and in 1721 married Sophia, daughter of Henry Harmanson by his wife Gertrude, daughter of Col. Southey Littleton. He died in 1752. His son, Littleton Tazewell, resided in Brunswick county and was a churchwarden and vestryman of the parish. One of his descendants was Littleton Waller Tazewell, Governor of Virginia.

FEILDING. Northumberland county.

Arms: Or, a lion rampant gules; also, argent on a fess azure three lozenges or.

The lion seal was used by Edward Feilding (son of Ambrose) on a letter of attorney in Sept., 1684, and both coats are given in a drawing made from Feilding silver in 1792, then in the possession of a descendant of Ambrose Feilding.

The Feildings of Northumberland appear in that county in 1662 in the person of Richard Feilding, a merchant from Bristol, England. He bought several large tracts of land in this county, and besides, owned a share in the ship "Phoenix," and in a mercantile business at Bristol with his brother, Edward. Richard Feilding died in 1666 unmarried. He left a plantation of a thousand acres, with all stock, servants, household goods, etc., to his brother, Ambrose Feilding, who came out to take possession of his Virginia place in 1667. He was a King's Justice from June 23, 1669, to Feb. 4, 1675. Ambrose Feilding's will was probated November 17, 1675, and devised his property to sons, Richard, Edward, and daughter Ann. Wife Ann received money for a mourning ring. In the inventory of his personal estate he is designated as "Mr. Ambrose Feilding of Wickocomico Hall, gent." This inventory names a good lot of household furniture contained in a five-room house and a two-room detached kitchen; included in this list were eighteen silver spoons and seven larger pieces of plate, two of which were marked with "ye Ffeilding Armes."

Of the sons of Ambrose Feilding, Richard died unmarried; and Edward took a more or less prominent part in county affairs till the time of his death in 1696. He appears first as a Justice March 19, 1679, and last on Sept. 12, 1683. He left four sons and two daughters, who have many descendants in Virginia, Kentucky, Alabama, Arkansas, and Texas.

All the original Feilding papers on file in the Northumberland Clerk's office were destroyed in the Civil War, but an old letter of Attorney, signed by Edward Feilding in Sept., 1684, is now owned by a descendant; this old letter bears a seal showing a lion rampant gules on a field or. This is the old Hapsburg seal of the principal family of Feilding in England—the Feildings of "Newham Paddox," Warwickshire, who were created Earls of Denbigh in 1620. This old letter of Attorney also bears the seal of Thomas Hobson, who was Clerk of Northumberland county from 1664 to 1716, Justice of the County Court, etc., and who has descendants yet in this country. This seal shows a three-masted ship under full sail, with prow pointed to the sinister side. In 1792 a descendant of Ambrose Feilding in Spotsylvania county, Va., made a drawing from old Feilding silver then in her possession, and sent it in a letter to her brother, who had gone to Kentucky to live. This drawing and letter are now owned by recipient's great grandson—Dr. J. L. Miller, Thomas, West Va., and shows two shields, one with the lion rampant and the other with the gold lozenges on a blue fess.

WOODHOUSE. Princess Anne county.

Arms: Quarterly ermine and azure, in the 2nd and 3rd quarters a leopard's head or.

Crest: A griffin's segreant or.

This old and distinguished Virginia family descends from Woodhouse of Waxham, Norfolk. John Woodhouse of this place had a son, Sir William, who married for his second wife, Elizabeth, daughter of Sir Philip Calthorpe and widow of Sir Henry Parker. A second son, Sir Henry Woodhouse, died in 1624, and by his marriage with Ann, daughter of Sir Nicholas Bacon, the Lord Keeper, and sister of Francis Bacon, first Lord Verulam, was father of Captain Henry Woodhouse, who was Governor of the Bermudas from Oct., 1623, to Jan. 13, 1626-7. Henry Woodhouse, son of Captain Henry, was born in 1607, and came to Virginia in 1637, settling in Lower Norfolk (now Princess Anne) county. He was Justice in 1642-3 and member of the House of Burgesses 1647 and 1652. He died in 1655, leaving several daughters and four sons, Henry, Horatio, John and William, who have numerous descendants.

BENNETT. Nansemond county.

Arms: Gules a bezant between three demi lions rampant argent.

Crest: Out of a mural coronet or, a lion's head gules, on the neck a bezant.

Richard Bennett was a nephew of Edward Bennett, a wealthy merchant of London and member of the Virginia Company. Richard Bennett was a member of the House of Burgesses in 1629 and 1631, and member of the Council 1642-9, removing in the latter year to Maryland. He returned to Virginia and in 1651 was appointed by Parliament one of the Commissioners to reduce Virginia and Maryland. He was Governor of the Colony from 30 April, 1652, to March, 1655. In 1658 he was again a member of the Council. In 1666 he was a Major-General of Militia, and in the "Sainsbury Abstracts" we find that in that year Thomas Ludwell, writing to Bennett, Lord Arlington, states that Major-General Bennett bore his (Arlington's) arms, and was he believed of his family. His will is dated 15 March, 1674, and was proved in Nansemond 12 April, 1675. He married Mary Ann Utie, and they had issue: (1) Richard of Greenbury Point, Maryland, who was drowned shortly before his father's death, leaving issue; (2) Anne Bennett, married, 1st, Theodorick Bland of Westover, 2nd, Colonel St. Leger Codd of Northumberland county, Va., and afterward of Maryland. She died 1687. (3) A daughter, married Col. Charles Scarborough of Accomac county, Va.

Robert Bennett, a brother of Edward Bennett of London, also came to Virginia prior to January, 1623-4, and in 1648 Mr. Philip Bennett, administrator of Robert Bennett, had a grant of land in Nansemond county.

NICHOLSON.

Arms: Azure on a cross argent between four suns ppr., a cathedral gules.

Crest: A demi-man habited in a close coat azure, buttons and cuff turned up or, face and hands ppr., armed with a head piece and gorget argent. In dexter hand a sword erect ppr., hilt and pommel of the second; in sinister an open Bible, clasps argent.

Motto: Deus mihi sol.

Sir Francis Nicholson of Downham Park, Yorkshire, was born in 1660; received an ensign's commission in the army 9 June, 1678; made lieutenant 6 May, 1684; Lieutenant-Governor of Virginia 1690; Governor of Maryland Jan., 1694; in 1698 returned to Virginia and remained there until 1705; in 1713 was made Governor of Acadia, and in 1719 Governor of South Carolina. He was knighted in 1720, returned to England in June, 1725, and died in London 5 March,

1728. He was one of the founders of William and Mary College, of which he was one of the first trustees.

COCK. Lancaster and Middlesex counties.

Arms: Argent a chevron engrailed gules between three eagle's heads erased sable, on a canton azure an anchor or.

In 1653 there is a patent to Nicholas Cock for 600 acres in Lancaster county, and in 1663 a grant to Maurice Cock, son of the above, of a like amount. In 1683 there is a grant recorded to Nicholas Cock of 346 acres in Middlesex. It is evident that Nicholas Cock was a Dutch settler, as he was naturalized with Minor Doodes and other Dutchmen in Middlesex in 1673. He died 25 Oct., 1687, and his tombstone in Middlesex bears the above arms, which are those of Cocke of the counties of Lancashire and Cornwall. There was a Nicholas Cock of South Pederwyn, Cornwall, who was married to Elizabeth Lower, daughter of Ferdinando Lower of Lesaunt, Cornwall, and whose pedigree is given in the Visitation of Cornwall for 1620. It is possible that this Nicholas might have been the father of Nicholas who came to Virginia. During the period of the Civil War in England many Englishmen went to Holland and became Dutch subjects, and it is possible that Nicholas may have done the same and, after settling in Virginia, became once more an English subject. He married, about 1661, Jane, widow of Bartholomew Curtis. By her second husband she had issue, Jane Cock, who married Rice Jones, and a son, Maurice Cock, who married Elizabeth, widow of Doodes Minor, son of Minor Doodes. Maurice Cock made his will 15 May, 1696, and with him the male line of this family became extinct.

WILLOUGHBY. Elizabeth City county.

Arms: Or on two bars gules three water bougets argent.

Crest: A griffin argent.

According to family tradition, Thomas Willoughby, the Virginia immigrant, was a nephew of Sir Percival Willoughby of Wallaton. He was born in 1601 and, according to Hotten, came to the colony in 1610. He was a Justice of Elizabeth City in 1628, member of the House of Burgesses 1629-32 and of the Council 1644-46. He was a large land owner in Lower Norfolk county, which his descendants owned for many generations. His wife's name is not known, but he had an only son, Col. Thomas Willoughby, born in Va., 25 Dec., 1632, and educated at Merchant Taylors School, London. He married Sarah, daughter of Richard and Ursula (Bisshe) Thompson of Northumberland county. He died in 1672 and his widow, Sarah, in 1673, leaving children, Thomas and Sarah.

WORMELEY. Middlesex county.

Arms: Gules on a chief indented argent, three lions rampant sable.

The immigrant, Ralph Wormeley, was descended from Sir John de Wormeley of Hadfield, Yorkshire. He was a member of the Council and died in 1649. His son Ralph of "Rosegill," Middlesex county, born 1620, died 1665, member of the Council, married Agatha, daughter of Richard Eltonhead and widow of Luke Stubbins of Northampton county, Va., and she married, 3rd, Sir Henry Chicheley, Governor of Virginia. Ralph Wormeley, 3rd, born 1650, died 5 Dec., 1703, educated at Oxford, was Secretary of State in 1693 and President of the Council.

SKELTON. Goochland county.

Arms: Azure a fess or between three fleur de lis.

Crest: A peacock's head erased ppr. in the beak an acorn or, stalked and leaved vert.

James Skelton, a gentleman of wealth and social prominence, was living in St. James Parish, Goochland, in 1735. He married Jane Meriwether, a daughter of Francis Meriwether and his wife, Mary Bathurst, who was a descendant of the ancient family of English Bathursts. The Skelton arms are engraved on old silverware now in possession of the Skeltons of Kentucky, which were brought from Virginia, and is also found on the book plate of Reuben Skelton, son of James Skelton. James and Jane Skelton had issue: (1) Reuben, clerk of St. Paul's Parish, Hanover county; (2) Meriwether of Hanover county, d.s.p.; (3) Lucy; (4) Sally, who married Col. Thomas Jones of Hanover county; (5) Bathurst, who married in 1766, Martha, daughter of John Wayles, lawyer, of Charles City. He died in 1769, leaving one child, who died in infancy. His widow, Martha Skelton, married, 2nd, 1 Jan., 1772, Thomas Jefferson, who was afterward President.

TEMPLE. King William county.

Arms: Argent two bars sable each charged with three martlets or.

Crest: A talbot sejant sable, collared and lined or.

Motto: Flecti non frangi.

The first member of the Temple family who settled in Virginia was Joseph Temple, born 1666, married Ann Arnold in England. They lived at Presque Isle, King William county. Joseph was the son of William and the grandson of John Temple of Kingston Deverell. (See Burke's "Landed Gentry.") Joseph and Ann Temple had a son Joseph, who married Mary, daughter of Col. Humphrey Hill of King and Queen county, by whom he had issue.

FOOTE. Stafford county.

Arms: Vert a chevron between three martlets argent.

Crest: A lion's head erased.

Motto: Pendentim.

The Footes were an old family long settled in the county of Cornwall. In the register of St. Paul's Parish, Stafford county, Va., are the following entries concerning the family: "Richard Foote, son of John Foote, gent., was born at Cardenham, in the county of Cornwall, the 10th of August, Anno 1632. Was married the 19th day of Dec., 1657 to his beloved wife Hester, the daughter of Nicholas Hayward of London, grocer, who was born in Allhallows

Parish, the 24th day of March, 1639-40."

Richard Foote came to Virginia to manage the extensive business of Nicholas Hayward; he returned to England and there married the daughter, Hester. They had issue, the following children: (1) Samuel, born 25 Jan., 1659, died 1697; (2) Susannah, born 13 Aug., 1658; (3) Mary, born 1 Oct., 1662, died 1664; (4) John, born 27 March, 1665, died 1692 at Jamaica; (5) Richard (first of the family to settle permanently in Va.), born 31 Jan., 1666; (6) Elizabeth, born 27 Oct., 1668; (7) Mary, born 10 Jan., 1670; (8) Hester, born 8 Dec., 1672; (9) George, born 22 Oct., 1673; (10) Sarah, born 22 Oct., 1675, died an infant; (11) Sarah, born 27 June, 1676; (12) Francis, born 8 Jan., 1678, died 1697; (13) Henry, born 5 July, 1680; (14) Mathias, born 13 Dec., 1683, died an infant.

Richard Foote, the younger, born 1666, settled in Stafford county, Va., where he died 21 March, 1729. Owing to the destruction of the records his wife's name is unknown, but he had issue: (1) Richard, born 1704, Justice of Stafford in 1745, and who left issue; (2)George; (3) John, d.s.p.; (4) Hester, married John Grant of Prince William, gent.; (5) Elizabeth.

DAVISON. James City.

Arms: Argent a stag trippant ppr. attired or.

Crest: A stag courant or, shot through the neck with an arrow argent.

Christopher Davison was the Colonial Secretary for Virginia in 1621; he was born in Stepney, Middlesex, and was the son of William Davison, Secretary of State to Queen Elizabeth.

FOWKE. Westmoreland county.

Arms: Vert a fleur de lis argent, a mullet for difference.

Crest: An Indian goat's head erased argent.

The first of this family was Col. Gerard Fowke, an ex-Royalist officer, who came to Virginia in 1651 and settled in Westmoreland county, purchasing lands there in 1657 from Nicholas Meriwether. He was the sixth son of Roger Fowke of Breward and Gunston Hall, Staffordshire. He died in 1669. An old deed, now in the possession of his descendants, has impressed upon it the above arms. He was a Burgess for Westmoreland county in 1663, and in 1664 moved to Maryland, near Port Tobacco, where he took up large grants of land. In 1665 he was a member of the Maryland Assembly and Colonel of Militia for Worcester county. His wife, whom he married in England, was named Ann ———, and they have left numerous descendants in the South.

MERCER. Stafford county.

Arms: Or on a fess between three crosses pattee gules in chief, and a mullet azure in base, as many bezants.

John Mercer of Marlborough, Stafford county, founder of the family in Virginia, was the son of John Mercer of Dublin, Ireland, and the great grandson of Noel Mercer of Chester, England. He was born 6 Feb., 1704, came to Virginia in 1720, and died 14 Oct.,

1763. He was a lawyer and large landed proprietor. He married, 1st, Catherine, only daughter of Col. George Mason, 2nd, by whom he had issue, and, 2nd, Elizabeth, daughter of the Rev. John Waugh. She was born in 1707 and died in 1750.

NICHOLSON. York county.

Crest: Out of a ducal crown, an arm grasping a battle axe.

The above crest is engraved on a silver tankard, formerly the property of Dr. Robert Nicholson of Yorktown, who married Elizabeth, daughter of Dudley Digges, member of the Committee of Safety. It is now in the possession of a descendant, Mrs. Sally Nelson Robins of Richmond.

SKIPWITH. Prince George county.

Arms: Argent three bars gules, a greyhound in full course in chief, sable, collared or.

Crest: A turnstile ppr.

Motto: Sans Dieu je ne puis.

The Virginia family descend from the Skipwiths of Prestwould in Leicestershire. Sir Henry Skipwith, Knight of Prestwould, was created a Baronet 20 Dec., 1622. His eldest son, Sir Henry, died single, and was succeeded by his brother, Sir Grey, who settled in Virginia. His son, Sir William, married Sarah, daughter of John Peyton. His eldest son, Sir Grey, born 1705, died without issue and the title devolved upon his brother Sir William, born 1707, died 1764, who married Elizabeth, only daughter of John Smith, High Sheriff of Middlesex. Their eldest son, Sir Peyton, 7th Baronet, married Ann, daughter of Hugh Miller. The descendants of the Skipwith family are still numerous in the South.

STEPTOE. Lancaster county.

Arms: Azure a fleur de lis argent.

Crest: Out of a ducal coronet or, a stag's head ppr.

Motto: Spes mea in Deo.

The immigrant was Anthony Steptoe, who was in Lancaster county in 1697. His son, Capt. John Steptoe, married Elizabeth, widow of John Eustace, they had issue: (1) William, who married Ann ———, and settled in Northumberland county; (2) John, who married Jane Lawson 12 June 1727; (3) James, who settled in Westmoreland county and was vestryman of Cople Parish in 1755. He married, first, Elizabeth Eskridge, daughter of George Eskridge, and, 2nd, Elizabeth, widow of Capt. William Aylett, by whom he had four sons. On the tomb of Philip Steptoe at Teddington, on the James River, is cut the above arms.

BALL. Lancaster county.

Arms: Argent a lion passant sable, on a chief of the second, three mullets of the first.

Crest: Out of the clouds ppr. a demi lion rampant sable, powdered with estoiles argent, holding a globe or.

Motto: Coelumqui tueri.

The above arms are from a painting on vellum which was brought to Virginia by the immigrant, William Ball. He was born in 1615 and died at "Millenbeck," Lancaster county, in 1680; married in London 2 July, 1638, to Hannah Atherold. They had issue: (1) Richard, died young; (2) William, born 2 Jan., 1641, who had issue; (3) Joseph, born 25 May, 1649, married and had issue; (4) Hannah, born 12 March, 1650. The descendants of the above have intermarried with the most prominent families of Virginia. Mary, daughter of Col. William Ball of Lancaster, being the mother of General George Washington.

MONTAGUE. Nansemond and Lancaster counties.

Arms: Argent three fusils in fess gules, between as many pellets.

Crest: A griffin's head couped, wings elevated or.

Motto: Disponendo me, non mutando me.

This family can trace descent from Drogo de Monteacuto, who came with William of Normandy to England in 1066. The Virginia immigrant, Peter, was a son of Peter and Eleanor Montague of Boveney, Parish of Burnham, Bucks, and was born in 1603. His mother was a daughter of William Allen of Burnham. His uncle, William Montague was a Fellow of Kings College, Cambridge, and Richard Montague, Bishop of Norwich, was his father's cousin. Peter Montague came to Virginia at the age of eighteen years. In 1627 he patented 150 acres in Upper Norfolk county, what is now Nansemond, and of which he was a Burgess in 1652 and 1653. He also owned considerable land in Lancaster and represented that county in the House of Burgesses from 1651 to 1658. His will, dated 27 March, 1659, was probated 25 May of that year. He mentions his wife Cicely, and sons, Peter and William, his three daughters, Ellen, Margaret and Elizabeth, and the child of Ann, late wife of John Jadwin.

CORBIN. King and Queen county.

Arms: Sable on a chief or three ravens ppr.

Thomas Corbin of Hall End, Warwickshire, born 24 May, 1594, died June, 1637, buried at Kingswinford; married in 1620, Winifred, daughter of Gawin Grosvenor of Sutton Coldfield, Warwickshire. Their third son, Henry Corbin, born in 1629, came to Virginia in 1654, and died 8 Jan., 1675. He first settled in Stratton Major Parish, King and Queen county, but also owned land in Lancaster, Westmoreland and Middlesex. He was Burgess for Lancaster in 1659, Justice for Middlesex in 1673, and Member of the Council in 1663. He married 25 July, 1645, Alice Eltonhead, daughter of Richard Eltonhead of Lancashire, England. His son, Gawin Corbin, was Burgess in 1700, 1702, 1718 and 1736, and also member of the Council. He died 1 Jan., 1745.

CARTER. Lancaster county

Crest: On a chapeau gules turned up ermine, a heron argent, beaked, legged and ducally gorged or.

The above seal is used on the original will of Thomas Carter, gent., recorded in Lancaster county, August, 1700, also on a deed in Spotsylvania county, made by Joseph Carter in 1739, a grandson of Thomas, and it is also used on the will of another grandson, Dale Carter, gent., recorded in Lancaster county in 1776. By referring to the Dale pedigree and arms it will be seen that the above is not a Carter crest, but the crest of Catherine Dale, his wife, who was a daughter of Edward Dale and his wife Diana Skipwith, sister of Sir Grey Skipwith, Bart., and daughter of Sir Henry Skipwith, Bart., of Prestwould, Leicestershire, England.

In 1653 there appeared in Lancaster county, Mr. Thomas Carter, who paid tithes upon himself and four servants. His home plantation was one he had purchased from Col. John Carter of Corotoman. It is not known, however, that there was any relationship between them. Thomas Carter was Justice in 1683 and in 1670 Deputy Clerk of the county, his father-in-law, Edward Dale, being Clerk from 1655 to 1674. Sometime prior to 1674 he married Catherine Dale, by whom he had six sons and two daughters: (1) Edward Carter, the eldest son, died in Lancaster in 1743, leaving sons, Thomas and William, and a wife, Elizabeth; (2) Thomas Carter, second son, inherited the plantation on Corotoman River. He was a Justice from 1704 to 1728 and a Captain in the Militia. He died in 1733, leaving a wife, Arabella, and eight sons and two grandsons; (3) Henry Carter, third son, was a Justice from 1728 to 1740 and a vestryman of Christ Church until his death. He married prior to 1700, Anne Harris, daughter of Gany Harris, gent. He died in 1743, leaving five sons and three daughters. (4) James Carter, fourth son, removed to Stafford county, where he died 24 Oct., 1743. He married in 1724, Mary, daughter of Hugh Brent of Lancaster county, and left six sons and one daughter. (5) Peter Carter, fifth son, inherited a plantation in St. Mary's parish, Lancaster county from his grandfather, Edward Dale, where he lived and died in 1721. He left a second wife named Margaret, and two sons and two daughters, one of each by each wife. (6) Joseph Carter, the youngest son, inherited a plantation in St. Mary's Parish from his grandfather Dale, where he lived until his death in 1759. His wife's name was Anne, and they had at least three sons and a daughter. He was a Justice in 1729, and in 1741 High Sheriff. (7) Elizabeth Carter, the elder daughter, married William George, who died in 1709, leaving several children. Thomas Carter, Sr., had also a son John, and a daughter Catherine.

GOOKIN. Lower Norfolk county.

Arms: Gules a chevron ermine between three crosses or.

Capt. John Gookin came to Virginia at a very early period. He was a brother of Daniel Gookin, who left Virginia in 1644 and settled at Roxbury, Mass., and the above arms are found on the tomb of Daniel Gookin, Jr., son of Daniel, who died at Cambridge, Mass. in 1686-7. Capt. John Gookin was a member of the Assembly from Lower Norfolk in 1639, and died 2 Nov., 1643. He married Sarah

Offley, the widow of Lieut.-Col. Adam Thorougood, and she afterwards married Francis Yeardley, son of Gov. Sir George Yeardley. By his wife Sarah, Capt. Gookin had a daughter Mary, who married William Moseley 2nd, she afterwards married Col. Anthony Lawson.

NEWTON. Westmoreland county.

Arms: Sable two shinbones salterways, the sinister surmounted of the dexter or.

Crest: A lion rampant argent.

The Virginia Newtons claim descent from the Newtons of Barr's Court, Gloucestershire. John Newton was in Westmoreland county in 1672. His will was probated 28 July, 1697, in it he leaves land at Carlton and Camelford, Yorkshire, Eng., to his son John, and also the house at Hull, "which was my father's," he also leaves land to his son John and his said son's four children; to son Joseph and his three sons; to son Benjamin and his daughter; to son Gerrard; to daughter Elizabeth Newton; to son Thomas; to wife Rose Newton; to grandson John, son of Joseph Newton. The will of Rose Newton, the wife of the immigrant, was probated in Westmoreland county 28 Jan., 1712, and from a deposition taken in 1709, she states that she was "aged 80 years" and the widow of John Newton, Sr.

LEFTWICH. New Kent county.

Arms: Azure three garbs or on a fess engrailed argent.

Crest: Five leaves conjoined at base vert.

Motto: Ver non semper floret.

The Virginia immigrant was Ralph Leftwich, who received grants of land as early as 1658. Owing to the destruction of the New Kent and Caroline county records, a gap occurs in the pedigree of at least two generations. The arms borne by the descendants of Augustine Leftwich are the same as those of Leftwich, county of Cheshire.

WISE. Accomac county.

Arms: Sable three chevronels ermine.

Crest: A demi-lion rampant gules, guttee d'eau, holding in the dexter paw a mace or.

The first of this family in Virginia was John Wise, a descendant of the Wise family of Sydenham, Devonshire. He sailed from Gravesend, England, 4 July, 1635, and settled in Accomac, then Northampton county. When Accomac was formed from this county in 1662, he was one of the Justices. Major John Wise, one of the old clerks of Accomac county, was the oldest son of Col. John Wise and his wife Margaret Douglas, she being the daughter of Col. George Douglas, a native of Scotland, who settled in Accomac, a descendant of the famous Earls of Angus. This Col. John Wise died in 1770. He was Colonel of Militia, a Justice and County-Lieutenant. The son, Major John Wise, represented Accomac in the House of Delegates, 1790, and in 1798 and 1799 he was Speaker of the House. He was Commonwealth Attorney in 1805, and was afterward Clerk of the Court, holding that office until his death, 30 March, 1812. He was twice married, his first wife being Mary Henry, daughter of Judge James Henry of Northumberland county. By her he had four sons, two of whom died in infancy. He married secondly, Sarah Corbin Cropper, daughter of General John Cropper, by whom he had five sons and one daughter.

FONTAINE. King William county.

Arms: D'azur au. chevron acc. en chef de deux trefles, et en p. d'une garbe, le tout d'or.

The Virginia branch of this family is descended from the noble family of De La Fontaine, Maine, France. John de la Fontaine was born about 1500 and held a commission in "Les Ordonnances du Roi," in the household of Francis I., retaining his commission during the succeeding reigns of Henry II. and Francis II. and until the second year of Charles IX. He and his father became converts to Protestantism about 1535. John De La Fontaine and his wife were murdered during the troublous period of 1563. They had four children, but only the names of two are known, viz: (1) James, aged about 14 in 1563. (2) Abraham, aged about 12 in 1563. James died in 1633 and left issue, a son, the Rev. James Fontaine, who went to London and married a Miss Thompson in 1628, by whom he had issue: (1) Jane. (2) Judith. (3) James, who became a Protestant minister in Germany. (4) Elizabeth. (5) Rev. Peter, who settled in London. (6) Francis d.s.p. The Rev. James Fontaine married, secondly, in 1641, Marie Chaillon of Pons, in Sainfonge, who died in 1678, aged 63 years, by her he had issue: (1) Susan. (2) Peter. (3) Mary. (4) Ann. (5) Rev. James, born at Jenouille, France, 7 April, 1658, married at Barnstaple, England, 8 Feb., 1686, to Anne Elizabeth Boursiquot, who died 29 Jan., 1721 at Dublin, Ireland. By her he had issue: (1) James, born 1686, who arrived in Virginia in Oct., 1717. (2) Aaron, born 1688. (3) Mary Anne, born 1690, died 1755 in Virginia, married 1716 in Dublin, Ireland, Matthew Maury of Castel Mauron, Gascony, came to Va. 1718. (4) Moses, born 1694. (5) Elizabeth, born 1701. (6) Rev. Peter, born 1691, married 1714, Elizabeth Fourreau; married, 2nd, E. Wade, and in 1716 came to Virginia and became rector of King William and Westover parishes. (7) John, born 1693, died in England. (8) Rev. Francis, born 1697, came to Va. and was Professor in William and Mary College and rector of York-Hampton parish.

WYCHE. Surry county.

Arms: Azure a pile ermine.

Crest: A dexter arm embowed, habited gules, turned up or, holding in the hand ppr. a sprig vert.

Motto: Malgre le tort.

The Virginia line trace descent from Wyche of Davenham, Cheshire, and from the ancient house of Wyche of Alderly, A. D.

1200. (1) William Wyche of Davenham married about 1475, Margery, daughter and co-heiress of Richard Brett. (2) Richard, married Mary, daughter of John Beeston of Beeston Castle. (3) Richard, born 1525, died 1595, married Margaret Houghton. (4) Richard of London, born 1554, married 1583, Elizabeth, daughter of Sir Richard Saltonstall, Lord Mayor, 1598. (5) Rev. Henry Wyche, M. A., Cambridge, Rector of Sutton, Surrey, bapt. 1604, died 1678, married Ellen, daughter of Ralph Bennett of Old Palace Yard, Westminster. (6) Henry Wyche, eldest son of above, born 4 Nov., 1645, came to Virginia and settled in Surry county, will proved there 18 March, 1714, and, acording to same, he had the following children: Eleanor, William, George, Sarah, Henry and James. William Wyche, son of above, lived in Surry county, will probated 15 Feb., 1720. Henry Wyche, son of the immigrant, moved to Brunswick county, will probated 1740. James, son of the immigrant, resided in Surry county, will probated 1749.

HONE. James City county.

Arms: Sable a leopard's head erased between three mullets argent.

Major Theophilus Hone, Justice of Warwick county in 1652, removed to Jamestown, where he was Burgess in 1666, and Sheriff in 1676. He married prior to 1672, the widow of William Richardson. The Virginia family claim descent from the Hones of Essex. Major Theophilus being the third son of Thomas Hone of Farnham, who married Judith, daughter of Theophilus Aylmer, Archdeacon of London.

EPPES. Charles City county.

Arms: Per fesse gules and or, a pale counterchanged, three eagles displayed of the last.

Crest: On a chaplet vert flowered or, a falcon rising of the last.

The above arms are on documents in the possession of the Eppes family and is also engraved on old silver which has been in the family for many generations. The arms correspond with Eppes of Canterbury. Lieut.-Col. Francis Eppes was in Virginia in 1635, bringing with him three sons, John, Francis and Thomas. The Eppes of Prince George are descended from Thomas, through Col. Peter Eppes, and the Nottoway branch also descend from Col. Peter. Francis Eppes, son of the immigrant, settled in what is now Chesterfield. He was born about 1628 and died in 1678. He married Elizabeth, widow of William Worsham of Henrico county, by whom he had four children. The descendants of Col. Francis Eppes are very numerous in Virginia.

PEYTON. Gloucester county.

Arms: Sable a cross engrailed or.

Crest: A griffin sejant or.

Motto: Patior potior.

Major Robert Peyton of Rougham, Norfolk, and of Isleham, Gloucester county, Virginia, was born in 1640 and died 1694. He was a son of Thomas Peyton and Elizabeth Yelverton, a daughter of Sir William Yelverton, Bart., of Rougham, Norfolk. He married in 1668 and was in Virginia before 1679. He was Major of the Gloucester County Militia. He had the following issue: (1) Elizabeth, born ante 1670, married Col. Peter Beverley. (2) Thomas, born about 1675, married Frances Tabb. (3) Robert, born 1680, married Mary ————. Sir John Peyton, son of Thomas and Frances (Tabb) Peyton, was born in 1710 and died 1790. He had issue, Thomas, born 1751, married Anne, daughter of Henry Washington. (2) Frances, born 1753, married John Tabb of Clay Hall, Amelia county. (3) Elizabeth, born 1756, married John Dixon, Jr., of Gloucester county. (4) Mary, born 1758, married Mordecai Throckmorton. (5) Harriett, born 1761, married Thacker Washington. (6) Seigniora, born 1767, married Thomas Tabb of Bolling. (7) Martha. (8) Henry Yelverton, born 1770. (9) John, born 1775, married Mary Chiswell, daughter of Warner Lewis. Sir John Peyton of Virginia became heir to the Baronetcy in 1721 through the death of Sir John Peyton of Isleham, England.

The Peytons of Westmoreland county are of kin to those of Gloucester county and use the same arms, with the addition of "a mullet argent, in the second quarter, and a bordure ermine" for a difference. Henry Peyton of Lincoln Inn died in London in 1656 and was a cadet of the Peytons of Isleham. He had issue, Robert born 1624; Valentine, Henry, Laurence, Catherine, Margaret, Henry, John, Charles and Mary. Of these, Valentine, Lawrence, Henry and John came to Virginia. Valentine died in Westmoreland county in 1665 at his estate of Nominy. Henry, his brother, died in 1659, and from these two brothers came a numerous progeny whose descendants are found through Virginia and the South.

ROOTES. King and Queen county.

Arms: Quarterly 1st and 4th, between three buglehorns, a chevron on which three arrows, points downwards, 2nd and 3rd, on a cross five pheons.

The above arms are on the bookplate of Philip Rootes, the elder, of "Rosewall," King and Queen county. They do not correspond in any degree to the arms given to Rootes in the Heralds College, which are "or three lozenges gules."

Philip Rootes, gent., the earliest ancestor to whom the family of that name in Virginia has been traced, lived at "Rosewall." The first mention of him is in a deed dated 1729, wherein the trustees of the town of Fredericksburg convey to Susannah Livingston, widow, a lot, and after her death to descend to Philip Rootes. In the vestry book of Stratton-Major he is referred to as "Captain," and he was a vestryman and churchwarden during the years from 1732 to 1751. In 1756 he is called "Major Philip Rootes." He owned estates in New Kent, Spotsylvania, Orange and Culpeper counties, and valuable property in Fredericksburg.

Major Philip Rootes was born about 1700 and his will was proved 12 Oct., 1756. He married Mildred, born about 1703, the daughter of Thomas Reade of Gloucester county, by whom he had the following children: (1) Philip; (2) Thomas Reade; (3) John; (4) George; (5) George; (6) Mildred; (7) Elizabeth; (8) Priscilla; (9) Mary; (10) Lucy. An extended pedigree of the family is given in "Rootes of Rosewall," by W. Clayton-Torrence.

FAIRFAX. Fairfax county.

Arms: Or three bars gemelles gules, surmounted of a lion rampant sable.

Crest: A lion passant guardant sable.

Supporters: Dexter, a lion guardant sable; sinister, a bay horse.

Motto: Fare Fac.

This family was seated at Towcester in Northumberland at the Conquest. The pedigree begins with Richard de Fairfax, son of John and grandson of Henry of Shapenbeck, who in 1204 possessed the Manor of Askham and other lands in Yorkshire. Sir Nicholas Fairfax died in 1570 leaving a son, Sir William, whose son, Sir Thomas, was created in 1629 Viscount Fairfax of Emely, in the peerage of Ireland. Of the same family, Sir Guy Fairfax was appointed Judge of the Court of King's Bench in 1478, his son Sir William, was Judge of the Court of Common Pleas in 1510, his son, Sir William, as High Sheriff of York in 1518. Thomas, eldest son of above, was Sheriff of Yorkshire in 1571 and knighted in 1576. Thomas, the eldest son of above, born in 1560, fought in the Low Country Wars, and was knighted by Lord Essex, and on 18 Oct., 1627, was created Baron Fairfax of Cameron in the Peerage of Scotland. He married in 1582, Ellen, daughter of Robert Aske of Aughton, and died 1 May, 1640. Ferdinando succeeded his father as second Baron. Thomas, eldest son of above, third Baron, was born 1611-12 and married in 1637 Anne, daughter of Lord Vere of Tilbury. Henry, fourth Lord Fairfax, married Frances, daughter of Sir Robert Barwicke. Thomas, fifth Lord Fairfax, married Catherine, daughter of Thomas, Lord Colepeper. Thomas, sixth Lord Fairfax, removed in 1747 to Virginia, and alienated his English estates in favor of his brother Robert, and built "Belvoir" and "Greenway Court" in Va. He d.s.p. 9 Dec., 1781. William Fairfax, son of Henry and Anne (Harrison) Fairfax, was born in 1691; was Virginia agent of his cousin, the sixth Lord Fairfax; married, 1st, in 1723, Sarah, daughter of Major Walker of the Bahamas; married, 2nd, Deborah Clarke of Salem, Mass., and died in 1757; his son Bryan succeeded as eighth Lord Fairfax. Thomas, eldest son of the eighth Lord, born in 1762, succeeded his father in the title. Albert, eldest son of the ninth Lord, had Charles Snowden Fairfax, tenth Lord, d.s.p. in 1869, being succeeded by his brother, Dr. John Contee Fairfax he being succeeded by his eldest son Albert Kirby Fairfax, born 23 June, 1870, twelfth and present Baron Fairfax.

HARWOOD. Warwick county.

Arms: Argent a chevron between three stags' heads cabossed sable.

Crest: A stag's head cabossed sable, holding in its mouth an oak bough ppr. acorned or.

The first of this family to arrive in Virginia was Capt. Thomas Harwood, who, in 1620, was "Chief of Martin's Hundred." He is believed to have been connected with Sir Edward Harwood, who was a member of the Virginia Company. He was a member of the Council and was Burgess for Mulberry Island 1629, 1630, 1633 and 1642, and for Warwick county 1644, 1645, 1648 and 1649; Speaker of the House 1648-9, and Member of the Council 1652. He was one of the most prominent men in the Colony and left numerous descendants living in Warwick and York counties. His son Humphrey Harwood, was Burgess for Warwick in 1685 and 1692. Thomas Harwood, probably a younger son of Capt. Thomas Harwood of Warwick, was a Justice of York in 1653.

LEE. York county.

Arms: Gules a fesse chequy azure and or between ten billets argent, four in chief, three, two and one in base.

Crest: On a staff raguly, lying fessways, a squirrel sejant ppr. cracking a nut; from the dexter end of the staff a hazel branch vert, fructed or.

Motto: Ne incautus futuri.

The Lee family, one of the most prominent in Virginia, descend from Lee of Coton, Shropshire.The first of the line was Col. Richard Lee, who was a Magistrate for York county in 1646, he also owned considerable property in Northumberland county. He died in Virginia, and his will was probated in London in 1664-5. He left a wife Anna, and the following issue: (1) John, born about 1645; (2) Robert, born about 1648; (3) Francis; (4) William; (5) Hancock; (6) Elizabeth; (7) Anne; (8) Charles. Col. Richard Lee was Secretary of the Colony in 1659 and one of the Privy Council.

TOWLES. Middlesex and Lancaster counties.

Arms: A lion passant.

The immigrant ancestor was Henry Towles, who settled first in Accomac county and married Anne Stokeley, member of an old family who settled at an early date on the Eastern shore of Virginia. Henry Towles afterward moved to Middlesex. He had issue, Henry, Jr., born about 1670,and Stokeley. born about 1695. In the Middlesex Clerk's office is a deed of Henry Towles, Sr., bearing a wax seal of the above arms. The arms cannot be located in the English Heraldic records under the name of Towles. Henry Towles, Jr., settled in Lancaster county. His wife was Hannah Therriot. His will was proved 12 June, 1734, and in it he mentions his children, Stokeley, Judith, Ann, Elizabeth and Jane.

READE. James City county.

Arms: Azure guttee d'or, a cross-crosslet fitchee of the last.

Crest: A shoveller close sable.

George Reade, Secretary of State for Virginia. was a descendant of the Reades of Faccombe, in the county of Southampton. In 1585 Andrew Reade purchased the manor of Linkenholt. Hampshire. His will was probated in 1623. His second son, Robert, married three times, his third wife being Mildred, daughter of Sir Thomas Windebanke. They had issue: (1) Andrew, D. D., of Lugershall, Wilts. (2) William. (3) Dr. Thomas, Fellow of New College, Oxford; Principal of Magdalen Hall, Oxford, 1643. (4) Robert, Secretary to Sir Francis Windebanke and living in 1669. (5) George, who came to Virginia in 1637, and in 1640 was Secretary of State pro tem., Burgess for James City county in 1649 and 1656. Member of the Council 1657-8, holding this office until his death in 1671. He married Elizabeth, daughter of Capt. Nicholas Martian of York county, and had at least seven children, viz: (1) Mildred, died 1694; (2) George d.s.p.; (3) Robert; (4) Thomas; (5) Francis; (6) Benjamin; (7) Elizabeth.

CARRINGTON. Cumberland county.

Arms: Sable on a bend argent three lozenges of the field.

Crest: Out of a ducal coronet or, a unicorn's head sable, armed and crested or.

The Virginia Carringtons descend from the ancient family of that name in Cheshire, England. The first of the name in this country was Colonel George Carrington, who settled at Boston Hill, Cumberland county, and was a son of Dr. Paul Carrington of the Island of Barbadoes. He married about 1732, when in his 21st year, Anne, the daughter of William Mayo, descended from another distinguished family. They both died in February 1785, and had issue, eleven children. Edward Carrington, their eighth child, born 11 Feb., 1748, died 10 Oct, 1810, was a most distinguished officer in the Revolution. He married Elizabeth Jacquelin Ambler. Another son of George Carrington was Judge Paul Carrington, who was a member of the Revolutionary Committee of Safety. His grandson, Colonel Henry A. Carrington, son of Henry and Louisa E. Carrington, was born in Charlotte county 13 Sept., 1832. His mother was a daughter of the Hon. William H. Cabell, Governor of Virginia from 1805 to 1808. Colonel Carrington was elected Clerk of the Circuit and County Courts of Charlotte in 1870, and continued in the office of County Clerk until his death in 1885. He was commissioned Lieut.-Col. of the 18th Virginia Infantry, and served in twenty-nine pitched battles, being three times wounded, and was taken prisoner at Gettysburg. One of his sons, John C. Carrington, is now the County Clerk for Charlotte.

CLAIBORNE. King William county.

Arms: Argent three chevronels interlaced in base sable, a chief and bordure of the last.

Crest: A dove and olive branch.
.Motto: Pax et copia.

This most distinguished family descend from Claiborn of the county of Westmoreland, of the Manor of that name which is mentioned in Doomesday Book, A. D., 1086. Col. William Claiborne, the Virginia immigrant, was born about 1587, and was the third son of Edmund Claiborne of Cleburne Hall, Yorkshire, and his wife Grace, daughter of Sir Alan Bellingham. He came to Virginia with Governor Wyatt in 1621 and in 1625 was appointed Secretary of State for the Colony and member of the Council, and held the latter place in 1627. On 6 April, 1642, he was appointed Treasurer of Virginia. He was a Justice for Accomac in 1631-2 and for York in 1633 and of Northumberland in 1653. He married twice, his first wife being Jane Buller of London, and his second, whom he married in Virginia, Elizabeth ————. He had known issue, three sons and one daughter: (1) William, who settled in King William county; (2) Thomas, who settled in King William county; (3) Leonard, who went to Jamaica, W. I., and died there in 1694; (4) Jane, married Col. Thomas Brereton of Northumberland county, and died before 20 May, 1671. Colonel William Claiborne died in 1676. His son, Leut.-Col. Thomas Claiborne, born 17 Aug., 1647, died 7 Oct., 1683, is buried at Romancoke, and his tomb bears the family arms.

BASSETT. New Kent county.
Arms: Or three bars wavy gules.
Crest: A unicorn's head couped argent.
Motto: Pro rege et populo.

Col. William Bassett, the son of William Bassett, yeoman, of Newport, Isle of Wight, came to Virginia previous to 1665, in which year he superintended the erection of a Fort at Jamestown. He resided at "Eltham" and was Burgess for New Kent county in 1692 and 1702; appointed to the Council 1707 and 1711; County Lieutenant of New Kent in 1707 and of King William in 1715. His tomb which is now at Hollywood Cemetery, Richmond, bears the above arms.

ARMISTEAD. Gloucester county.
Arms: Or a chevron between three points of spears sable, tasseled in the middle.
Crest: A dexter arm in armor embowed ppr. holding the butt end of a broken spear.
Motto: Suivez raison.

William Armistead of Virginia was the son of Anthony Armistead of Kirk Deighton, Yorkshire, and his wife Frances Thompson, whom he married in 1608. The son, William, was baptized in All Saints, Kirk Deighton, 3 August, 1610. He came to the Colony about 1635 and died before 1660. My his wife, Anne, he had issue: (1) William, d.s.p.; (2) John; (3) Anthony, ancestor of President Tyler; (4) Frances; (5) Ralph. Colonel John Armistead, second son, was Sheriff of Gloucester in 1675; member of the House of Burgesses 1685 and of the Council in 1687. Anthony Armistead was Sheriff of Elizabeth City 1684 and Burgess in 1699.

ATKINSON. Dinwiddie county.

Arms: Argent an eagle displayed with two heads sable, on a chief gules a rose between two martlets or.

Roger Atkinson of "Mansfield" came from Cumberland, England, to Virginia about 1750. He married Anne, daughter of John, second in descent from John Pleasants of "Curle's," Henrico county, who came from Norwich, England in 1665. John and Anne Atkinson had issue: (1) John, d.s.p; (2) Jane, married Gen. Joseph Jones; (3) Roger, married, 1st, Agnes Poythress; 2nd, Sally Spotswood; (4) Jane, married John Ponsonby; (5) Thomas, married Sally C. Page; (6) Robert, married Mary Tabb, daughter of William Mayo of Powhatan.

The above arms are engraved on an old silver salver formerly the property of Roger Atkinson and now in the possession of the Dutlow family of Charleston, W. Va. The arms are the same as those of Atkinson of Newcastle.

BOWLES.

The Bowles arms are quartered on the Lewis silver, the Bowles family settling in Maryland. The quartering is "Azure three standing bowls argent, out of each bowl issuing a boar's head or." The arms correspond with that of Bowles of Gosberkirk, Lincolnshire, and of Milton Hill, Abingdon.

HOWELL.

The Howell arms are quartered on the silver of the Warner Lewis family. The arms are "Gules three towers triple towered argent." They correspond with the arms of Howell of Monmouthshire,Wales.

CARTER. Lancaster county.

Arms: Argent a chevron between three cart wheels vert.

Crest: On a mount vert a greyhound sejant argent, sustaining a shield of the last charged with a cart wheel vert.

The immigrant of this family was John Carter, who, in 1649, was a member of the House of Burgesses for Upper Norfolk, and in 1654 from Lancaster county, and Commander-in-Chief of the forces sent against the Indians. He died in 1669. His first wife was Jane, daughter of Morgan Glynn, by whom he had George and Eleanor; he married, 2nd, Ann, daughter of Cleve Carter, by whom he had Charles and John, and by his third marriage to Sarah, daughter of Gabriel Ludlowe, he had Sarah and Robert. The Carter arms are found on a seal attached to a deed of Landon Carter 18 Sept., 1752, and they are found on the tombstone of Hon. Robert Carter at Christ Church, Lancaster; also on the tomb of Robert's wife, Judith Armistead; and also on that of the Hon. Mann Page, who died 1730, having married a daughter of the said Robert Carter.

PARKER.

Arms: Vert a chevron between three stags' heads cabossed or.

Crest: On a chapeau gules turned up ermine, a stag trippant ppr.

The family records of the Parkers of Browsholme, Yorkshire, England, show that two members, at least, of that family went to Virginia. The family descend from William Parker, Archdeacon of Cornwall, the second brother of Thomas Parker of Browsholme, Esqr. William Parker was Justice of Cornwall and had two sons, James, the eldest, marrying Katherine, eldest daughter of Sir Richard Buller of Shillingham, Cornwall, by whom he had twenty-one children. The Parker family removed from Yorkshire to Cornwall about 1580, and the pedigree of the Bullers, which shows the intermarriage of James Parker of "Blisland," is given in the Visitation of Cornwall in 1620. In the English records of the Parker family, entered under date 1st Sept., 1673, and in possession of descendants, is given: "Richard, the 9th son of James and Katherine Buller Parker, was Doctor of "Phyzicke," went into Virginy, married a Londoner and had issue, six children. Liveth upon St. James River in ye uplands of Virginy and hath been High Sheriffe of ye said county." "George, ye 13th child, prentice to a wollings draper at Hunginton, 12 myles of Exeter, went from there into Virginy." There was a George Parker who patented 450 acres of land in Northampton county 5 June, 1650, and 1,300 acres 30 March, 1655, there was also a Mr. Richard Parker who patented 400 acres in Nansemond county 5 Oct., 1654, and he also patented 350 acres on north side of James River in 1669. It seems quite probable that these were the two brothers above mentioned, there was, however, no Richard Parker who was a High Sheriff at that period, but George Parker was High Sheriff of Accomac county in 1656, and a member of the County Courts of both Accomac and Northampton. It is reasonable to suppose, therefore, that it was George Parker who was the High Sheriff and not his brother Richard, as given in the English records. While some of the Virginia Parkers (Northampton county) claim descent from the Parkers, Earls of Morley, the proof of such descent is not conclusive. Captain George Parker of Accomac lived at "Poplar Grove" and his will was proved in 1674.

TUCKER. Williamsburg.

Arms: Azure a chevron or between three seahorses of the second.

Crest: A lion's gamb erased gules holding a battle axe, the head argent and handle or.

Motto: Suspice Teucro.

St. George Tucker, son of Henry Tucker of Bermuda, W. I., was born at Port Royal, on that island, 27 June, 1752, and came to Virginia in 1771 to enter William and Mary College. After graduation he commenced the practice of law. He was Colonel of Militia in the Revolution; Judge of the General Court in 1787;

Professor of Law in William and Mary in 1789, and in 1813 a Judge of the U. S. Circuit Court. He married, 1st, 22 Sept., 1777, Frances, daughter of Theodorick Bland, Sr., of Prince George, and widow of John Randolph of "Mattoax," Chesterfield county; and 2nd, in 1791, Lelia, widow of George Carter and daughter of Sir Peyton Skipwith, but had no issue by the second marriage. He died 10 Nov., 1828. In the Church of St. Peter at St. George's, Bermuda, may be seen monumental inscriptions of the Tucker family bearing the above arms.

STROTHER. King George county.

Arms: Gules on a bend argent three eagles displayed azure.

Crest: A greyhound sejant or.

William Strother, the founder in Virginia of this family, is said to have emigrated from Northumberland, England. He settled on the Rappahannock River, near the present Port Conway, about 1673. His will was probated in Richmond county 4 Nov., 1702. He left a wife, Dorothy, and sons, William, James, Jeremiah, Robert, Benjamin and Joseph. An extended history of the Strother family will be found in "The Buckners of Virginia," edited by Wm. Armstrong Crozier, N. Y., 1907.

The family tradition has always been that the Virginia immigrant was of the Northumberland Strothers, and they have used the arms of that family.

THORNTON. Gloucester county.

Arms: Argent a chevron sable between three hawthorn trees ppr.

Crest: Out of a ducal coronet or, a lion's head ppr.

The arms used by the Virginia family are those of Thornton of Yorkshire, and the immigrant, William Thornton, is believed to have come from that county. He is mentioned as early as 1646 and in 1665 he received a grant of land in Gloucester county and was vestryman of Petsworth Parish in 1677. He had issue, three sons, William, Francis and Rowland. The son, William, was born 27 March, 1649, died 15 Feb., 1727. Like his father, he was a vestryman of Petsworth Parish. He married three times, and had sixteen children. Francis Thornton of Stafford county was born 5 Nov. 1651, and died 1726. His first wife was Alice, daughter of Capt. Anthony Savage of Gloucester, and by her had issue, seven children. He had no issue by his second wife. Rowland Thornton, third son of William, married Elizabeth, daughter of Alexander Fleming. He was dead in 1701, and it is thought left no issue.

STITH. Charles City county.

Arms: Argent a chevron engrailed between three fleurs de lis sable.

The first of this family in Virginia was Col. John Stith, who had a grant of land in Charles City county in 1663. He was a practising lawyer in 1680; Sheriff in 1691, and a member of the House of Burgesses in 1685, 1692 and 1693. His known children were:

(1) Anne, married Col. Robert Bolling of Kippax, Prince George.
(2) Col. Drury Stith, who had land in Charles City in 1703, Sheriff
in 1719-20 and 1724-5. He removed to Brunswick county about this
time and was first clerk of the county in 1732. He married Susannah, daughter of Launcelot Bathhurst, the second son of Sir Edward Bathhurst, who was knighted in 1643. Of the descendants of
Col. Drury Stith, at least eight became county clerks. (3) Capt.
John Stith, married Mary, daughter of William Randolph of Turkey Island, and sister of Sir John Randolph. Their son, Rev.
William Stith, born 1689, was a graduate of William and Mary
College. His theological studies were completed in England,
where he was ordained to the Episcopal Church. He was elected
master of the Grammar school at William and Mary in 1731, and
Chaplain to the House of Burgesses. In 1736 he was rector of
Henrico Parish and resided at "Varina," where he wrote his celebrated "History of Virginia." In 1752 he was President of William
and Mary College, and remained in that office until his death in
1755. He married his cousin Judith Randolph, by whom he had
three daughters. The arms given above, are taken from President
Stith's book-plate, and are also on a wax seal to a deed of con-
veyance. The Stith family are very prominent, not only in Virginia, but in Georgia, South Carolina and North Carolina. One of
the most prominent branches settling in the latter State are the
descendants of Dr. Buckner Stith, who settled in Rockingham
county in 1820. He married Lucinda, daughter of Capt. Thomas
Blackwell of the above county, who was for many years a member
of the Senate. They had issue, twelve children: (1) Washington
Lafayette, born 1827, d.s.p.; (2) Thomas Randolph, born 1829,
d.s.p.; (3) Laurence Augustine, born 1832, married Frances Jarvis;
(4) Virginia Caroline, born 1834, married Thomas C. Davis; (5)
Buckner Dade, born 1836; (6) Frances Rebecca, born 1838, married
Alpheus Brown; (7) Landonia, born 1840, d.s.p.; (8) Powhattan,
born 1841, d.s.p.; (9) Thomas Bertrand, born 1843, Lieut. in C. S. A.,
killed 1864; (10) Roberta Washington, born 1845, married a Tyler
of Va.; (11) Lucinda Cornelia, born 1848, married ———— Evans
of S. C.; (12) John Randolph, born 1857, d.s.p. Dr. Laurence Augustine Stith, third of above children, Surgeon in C. S. A., married 26 Jan., 1876, Frances, daughter of Moses W. Jarvis, and
Frances Blackwell, his wife, of New Berne, N. C. They had issue:
(1) Jarvis Wicksborn, born 1877; (2) Frances Blackwell, born
1878, married Elizabeth E. Bateman; (3) Charles Herbert, born
1880, married Cora Virginia Farley, by whom he has issue. Mary
Jarvis Stith, born 1901, and Laurence Augustine Stith, born 1904.
Extended notices of the Stith family are found in the "William
and Mary Quarterly," the "Richmond Critic of 1890" and Crozier's
"History of the Buckners of Virginia."

MINOR.

For arms and pedigree, see under Doodes.

MOREHEAD. Prince William county.

Arms: Argent on a bend azure three acorns or, in chief a man's heart ppr. within a fetterlock sable, the whole surrounded with an oak wreath ppr. acorned or.

Crest: Two hands conjoined grasping a two-handed sword ppr.

Motto: Auxilio Dei.

The first of this family was Charles Morehead, a Scottish gentleman, who settled in what is now Prince William county, in the early part of the eighthteenth century. He is known to have had at least one son, John Morehead, whose will was probated in Fauquier county, 24 Oct., 1768, in which he mentions sons, Charles, Joseph, John, Alexander, William, Samuel and Presley Morehead, and daughters, Mary Lawrence and Elizabeth Brixtraw. His son, Charles Morehead, a captain in the Revolution, died in Leeds Parish, Fauquier county, in 1783. His will mentions, son Turner, son Charles, sons Armistead, James and Presley; daughter Kerrenhappuch Morehead, and wife Mary. Joseph Morehead, grandson of Charles, the immigrant, moved to North Carolina, and married Elizabeth Turner, the daughter of James and Kerrenhappuch Turner of Maryland, whose sons and grandsons were with General Greene in the Revolution. Another daughter, Mary Turner, married Charles, the brother of Joseph Morehead, and left offspring in the West, of these, Governor Charles S. Morehead of Kentucky, and his cousin, Governor James Turner Morehead of the same State, have been eminent statesmen, serving not only as Governor, but also in the Senate of the U. S. from that State. The North Carolina branch has also produced the late Governor John M. Morehead, and his brother, Hon. James Turner Morehead, who, at one time, represented his District in Congress. Another descendant in the West is the Hon. Charles R. Morehead, some time Mayor of El Paso, Texas, who served with gallantry in the Mexican War. The Morehead arms are found on an old painting in possession of the North Carolina branch of the family.

WATERS. Elizabeth City.

Arms: Sable on a fess wavy argent between three swans of the second, two bars wavy azure.

Crest: A demi griffin azure.

Motto: Toujours fidele.

Edward Waters, gent., was born in England in 1584, came to Virginia and before 1622 married Grace O'Neil, who was born 1603. He held the rank of Captain; Burgess in 1625, and was Commander and Commissioner of Elizabeth City in 1628. He died in England, his will being made at Great Hornmead, Hertfordshire, 20 August, 1630, and proved the 18 Sept. of that year. He left to his son, William his lands in Virginia, mentions his brother John Waters of Middleham, Yorkshire; other legatees being his wife Mrs. Grace Waters, and his daughter Margaret. The son, William, was born in Virginia before 1624. He was Burgess for Northampton county in 1654, 1659 and 1660. He died about 1685, leaving issue, six sons, Richard, John, Edward, Thomas, Obedience and William. John and Richard settled in Maryland. John married Mary Maddox, and died in 1708, leaving a son, John. Richard Waters married Elizabeth, daughter of Col. Southey Littleton of Virginia. The above arms are used by the Maryland branch of the family.

ALEXANDER. Stafford county.
Arms: Per pale argent and sable a chevron, and in base a crescent all counterchanged.
Crest: A bear sejant erect ppr.
Motto: Per mare per terras.
According to the tradition in the family, which, however, has not been proven by documentary evidence, John Alexander, the first of the name in Virginia, was the fourth son of William Alexander, the Poet, and first Earl of Stirling, born 1580, died 1640, and married Janet Erskine, daughter of Sir William Erskine. John Alexander obtained a grant of 1,500 acres in Northampton county in 1659. In 1664 as John Alexander, Sr., he patented land in Westmoreland county. He died in 1677 and had issue, John, Robert and Philip. Robert Alexander, eldest son and heir at time of his father's decease, lived in Stafford county. He married Frances ———. He died before 1 June, 1704. He had sons, Robert, born 1688, died 1735, married Ann, daughter of Col. Gerard Fowke of Maryland, and who left issue, and Charles Alexander, who d.s.p.

HARRISON. Stafford county.
Arms: Azure three demi-lions rampant or.
Crest: A demi-lion rampant argent, holding a laurel branch vert.
The first of this line, which is distinct from the James River Harrisons, was Burr Harrison, who was baptized in England in 1637, died 1706, and married Mary, widow of Edward Smith. One of his sons, Thomas, born 1665, called Thomas of Chappawamsic, was Justice and Burgess for Prince William county from 1741 to 1746, in which year he died. His son, Col. Burr Harrison, born 1699, married 31 July, 1722, Ann Barnes, by whom he had issue, ten children. The above arms are on a seal attached to a deed at Stafford county given by Col. Burr Harrison. They are similar to the arms of the Harrisons of Westmoreland and Yorkshire.

HARRISON. Surry county.
Arms: Azure two bars ermine, between five estoiles, three, two and one, argent.
The immigrant was Benjamin Harrison, Clerk of the Council 1633 and Burgess in 1642. His son, Benjamin of "Wakefield," was a Justice of Surry 1671, Sheriff 1679, Burgess 1680 and 1682 and member of the Council from 1698 until his death 30 Jan., 1712-13. From his eldest son, Benjamin, descend the Harrisons of "Berkeley," and from the youngest, Nathaniel, the families of the name at "Brandon" and "Wakefield." The latter, Col. Nathaniel Harri-

son, married Mary, daughter of Hon. Cole Digges, born 1717, died 12 Nov., 1744, by whom he had four children: Nathaniel, born 1739, died 1740; Digges, born Oct., 1743, died Nov. of that year; Elizabeth, born 1737; Benjamin, born 1742. Upon the tomb of Mrs. Mary Harrison at Denbigh Church, Warwick county, are found the following arms: Dexter. Between two bars, five estoiles, three, two and one, for Harrison. Sinister—Five eagles displayed, for Digges. These arms are the same as Harrison of the counties of Essex and Kent, England.

AMBLER. York county.

Arms: Sable on a fesse or between three pheons argent, a lion passant guardant gules.

Crest: Two dexter hands conjoined sustaining a mural crown.

John Ambler of Yorkshire, England, Sheriff in 1651, married Elizabeth Baradike, and had, with other issue, a son, Richard, born 24 Dec., 1690, died 1766, who came to Virginia in 1716 and settled at Yorktown. He married Elizabeth, daughter of Edward Jacqueline of Jamestown. Richard Ambler's sister, Mary, married the Rev. George Shaw of Yorkshire, and was the grandmother of Charles Shaw Lefevre, Speaker of the House of Commons, and afterward raised to the dignity of Viscount Eversley. Richard and Mary Ambler had issue: (1) Elizabeth, born 1731; (2) Edward, born 1733; (3) John, born 1735; (4) Richard, born 1736; (5) Martha, born 1736 (twins); (6) Mary, born 1740; (7) Jacqueline, born 1742; (8) George, born 1744; (9) Richard, born 1748. Edward Ambler, born 1733, married Mary Cary, daughter of Wilson Cary. One of his sons was Col. John Ambler, born 1762, died 1836, and was Lieut.-Col. in the War of 1812. Upon his tombstone is a shield of arms, bearing those of Ambler, Cary and Jacqueline.

WILSON. Elizabeth City.

Arms: Sable on a cross engrailed between four cherubims or, a human heart of the first, wounded on the left side ppr. and crowned with a crown of thistles vert.

Capt. Willis Wilson, Burgess for Elizabeth City in 1692 and died 19 Nov., 1701, aged 28 years, was the son of Col. William Wilson and Jane, his wife. Col. Wilson died 17 June 1713, aged 67 years, and his wife 5 May, 1713, aged 53 years, and left an only surviving daughter. The tomb of Col. Wilson bearing above arms was formerly in the churchyard at Hampton, but was destroyed by Federal vandals during the War.

BYRD. Charles City county.

Arms: Argent a cross flory, between four martlets gules, on a canton azure a crescent of the field for difference.

Crest: A bird rising gules.

The Virginia branch descend from Byrd of Braxton, Cheshire. The immediate ancestor was John Byrd, goldsmith, of London, who married a sister of Thomas Stagg, who had settled in Virginia. His son William Byrd, born 1652, came to Virginia about 1674 and settled first in Henrico county. He was Justice, Sheriff, member of the House of Burgesses, in 1681 member of the Council, and in 1687 Auditor-General. In 1688 he removed to "Westover," Charles City county. He married Mary, daughter of Col. Warham Horsmanden of the Virginia Council, formerly of Purley, Essex. He died in 1704 and had issue: (1) Ursula, died 1698, married Robert Beverly; (2) Susan, married John Brayne of London; (3) a daughter; (4) a son; (5) Col. William Byrd of Westover, born 28 March, 1674, died 1744. The armorial bookplate of the second William Byrd is well-known to American collectors.

CARY. Warwick county.

Arms: Argent on a bend sable, three roses of the field leaved vert.

Crest: A swan ppr. wings elevated.

Mottoes: (1) Comme je trove. (2) Sine Deo careo.

The Carys descend from an ancient English family. William Cary, born about 1500, died 1572, was Mayor of Bristol in 1546. He had a son Richard, a merchant in Bristol, born 1525, died 1570, leaving a son, William, born 1550, died 1632, Mayor of Bristol in 1611. He had John Cary of Bristol, who married Alice, daughter of Henry Hobson, Alderman of Bristol, by whom an only son, Miles Cary, born 1620, came to Virginia in 1640. He settled in Warwick county, was a Colonel of Militia; Justice in 1652; Burgess in 1659 and member of the Council until his death 10 June, 1667. He married a daughter of Thomas Taylor of Warwick and had issue: (1) Major Thomas; (2) Ann; (3) Henry; (4) Bridget; (5) Elizabeth; (6) Col. Miles of "Ceeleys," born 1665, died 1708. The arms of Cary are on the tomb of the immigrant at Windmill Point, Warwick county.

BRANCH. Henrico county.

Arms: Argent a lion rampant gules oppressed by a bend sable.

Crest: Out of a ducal coronet or, a cock's head ppr. in its beak a branch vert.

According to a tradition in the family, the grandfather of the Virginia immigrant was Sir John Branch, Lord Mayor of London, circa 1485. Christopher Branch of "Arrowhallocks" and "Kingsland," Henrico county, was born about 1600. He came to Virginia with his wife Mary in March, 1619-20, and died about 1682. He had issue: (1) Thomas of Henrico, born April, 1623, died 1693, married Elizabeth, by whom he had issue; (2) William of Henrico, born about 1625, died 1676, married Jane ————, and had issue; (3) Christopher of Charles City county, born 1627, died 1665, and left issue. The descendants of the above three sons have become prominent in the history of the State.

CABELL. Henrico county.

Arms: Sable a horse rampant argent, bitted and bridled or.

Crest: An arm in armor embowed, grasping a sword all ppr.

Motto: Impavide.

William Cabell, born in England 9 March, 1699, was the son of Nicholas Cabell of Warminster and his wife, Rachel Hooper of Frome Selwood, and the grandson of William Cabell of Brooke, Esqr. William Cabell, graduated at the Royal College of Medicine, London, and afterward entered the Royal Navy as a surgeon. Resigning his commission, he came to Virginia about 1724. In 1726 he was a Deputy-Sheriff in St. James Parish, Henrico. He married Elizabeth Burks and had issue: (1) Mary, born 1726; (2) William, born 1730; (3) Joseph, born 1732; (4) John; (5) Nicholas, born 1750.

MOORE. King William county.

Arms: Ermine three greyhounds courant sable collared gules, and for augmentation on a canton gules, a lion passant.

The Moores of King William county descend from John Moore, who came to Virginia in 1620 at the age of 36. His wife, Elizabeth, came in 1622, and they were living in Elizabeth City in 1625. Their son, Augustine Moore, was living in 1676 and died before 1688. He married twice, his first wife being Anne, and his second Elizabeth. He had issue: (1) John; (2) Elizabeth, married Capt. John Goodwin; (3) Capt. Augustine, one of the Justices of Elizabeth City county. He probably married Mary Woolley, and had issue. John, Edward, Merritt, Daniel, Martha, Ann, William and Augustine. Daniel Moore, above, had a son Augustine located in King William county, and named his house "Chelsea," after the home of the celebrated Sir Thomas More. He died in 1743 and left issue, five children. The above arms are given on the authority of Campbell, the historian, and are taken from his "History of the Spotswood Family."

GRIFFIN. Rappahannock county.

The first of this family in Virginia was Thomas Griffin, who from 1651 received various grants of land. His wife was Sarah ——————. He died about 1660, his widow married, secondly, Samuel Griffin of Northumberland county. The children of Thomas and Sarah Griffin were: (1) Colonel Leroy Griffin of Rappahannock, born 1646 (deposition); (2) Thomas Griffin; (3) Winifred Griffin.

Colonel Leroy Griffin was Justice of Rappahannock in 1680. He married Winifred, daughter of Henry Corbin of "Buckingham," Middlesex county. Her will was probated in Richmond county in 1711. They had issue: (1) Thomas; (2) Corbin of Middlesex, Justice in 1700, will probated in 1701, married Judith, daughter of Christopher Wormeley of Middlesex, and d.s.p.; (3) Winifred, married Col. Peter Presley of "Northumberland House," Northumberland county. The latter's will was probated 10 Sept., 1750, and his only daughter and heiress, Winifred, married Anthony Thornton, and was mother of Colonel Presley Thornton of "Northumberland House," member of the Council 1760-69.

Thomas, son of Colonel Leroy Griffin and Winifred Corbin, received a grant of 3,136 acres in Richmond county in 1707. He was member of the House of Burgesses for that county in 1718 and 1723. He married Elizabeth ————, and his will was probated in 1733, and his wife's in 1761. They had issue: (1) Leroy of Richmond county, will probated in 1750, in which he mentions "five family pictures and a coat of arms." He was sheriff of the county in 1734, and married Mary Ann, only daughter and heiress of John Bertrand of "Belleisle," Lancaster county. (2) Winifred Griffin, married Capt. Samuel Peachey of Richmond county. (3) Alice Griffin, married Travers Colston. (4) Ann Griffin. married ———— Tarpley. (5) Sarah.

Note.—The editor has made every effort to obtain a description of the Griffin arms, but without success.

PAGE. Gloucester county.

Arms: Or a fess dancette between three martlets azure, within a bordure of the last.

Crest: A demi-horse per pale dancette or and azure.

Motto: Spe labor levis.

Francis Page, born 1594 died 1678, of Bedfont, Middlesex, England, had issue: (1) Matthew, settled in James City county, where he died in 1673, and had issue, Matthew, Luke and Mary, who married James Whaley. (2)Francis. (3) Robert of Hatton, Hounsley Heath, England, had a son John who came to Virginia. (4) Gibbs. (5) Ince. (6) John, born 1627 and died 1692. He was a member of the Council and married Alice Luckin. In his will he mentions two sons, Francis, born in 1657, he married Mary, daughter of Edward Digges and their daughter, Elizabeth, married her cousin, John, son of Robert Page above. Matthew Page, second son of John Page, the Councillor, was born at Williamsburg in 1659, and died in 1703, he was one of the Council from Gloucester county. He married about 1689, Mary, daughter of John Mann of Gloucester, and settled about 1700 at "Rosewell," which has since been the home of the Page family.

MERIWETHER. Albemarle county.

Arms. Or three martlets sable, on a chief azure a sun in splendor ppr.

Crest: An arm in armor embowed, in the hand a sword argent, hilt and pommel or, entwined with a serpent vert.

Motto: Vi et consilio.

The immigrant ancestor of this family was Nicholas, who was thought to have been born in Wales. He died in 1678, leaving issue, four sons: (1) Nicholas, born 1647, married Elizabeth, daughter of David Crawford of New Kent, by whom he had issue, nine children. He was a vestryman of St. Peters, New Kent, from 1685 to 1698. (2) Francis, married Mary Bathurst, daughter of Lancelot, and granddaughter of Sir Edward Bathurst. (3) David, married and had issue, one son. (4) William, married Elizabeth, daughter of John Bushrod of Westmoreland county. (5) Thomas, lived and died near Tappahannock, Essex county, his will was probated in 1708. The descendants of the above settled in what is now Albemarle county.

CRAWFORD. New Kent county.

Arms: Gules a fesse ermine.
Crest: An ermine argent.
Motto: Sine labora nota.

John Crawford, scion of an old Scottish family, and by tradition, said to have been of the line of the Earls of Crawford, came to Virginia about 1643. His son David was born in Scotland about 1625, and was granted land in James City county in 1667. He afterward moved to New Kent and patented land there in 1672. David 'had known issue: (1) Elizabeth, born about 1650, married Nicholas Meriwether; (2) a daughter, who married a Lewis; (3) Angelina, married a McGuire; (4) David, born about 1662, died 1762, aged 100 years; (5) John, died 13 Dec., 1689, and had a daughter, Angeline, who was baptized 2 Nov., 1689. The above arms are taken from the Crawford book-plate.

JADWIN. Rappahannock county.

Arms: Sable, ten plates, four, three, two and one, a chief or.
Crest: An oak tree vert, fructed or, supported by two lions' paws erased of the same, entwined with a scroll, inscribed with this motto: "Robur in vita Deus."

The first of this family in Virginia was John Jadwin who patented 650 acres on the south side of the Rappahannock 13 Nov., 1658. A pedigree of the family is given in the Visitation of London for 1634. The arms were exemplified by Sir William Segar, Garter King of Arms, to Robert Jadwyn of London, under date 1629. The family descend from William Jadwyn of Barwick, who had Thomas Jadwyn of London, gent., who married Lucy, daughter and heir of Sir John Skillicorne of Presthall, Lancashire. Their son, Robert of London, living in 1634, married Cisley, daughter of Sir Francis Clarke of London, Knt., by whom sons Robert and John. Robert Jadwyn had a son, John, who, as stated, went to Virginia. Thomas Jadwyn, above, married for his second wife, Elizabeth Rodway, widow, 28 May, 1594. (Par. Reg. of St. Mary Aldemary, London.) He was one of the Virginia adventurers and was present at several meetings of the Virginia Council in 1619. His will was probated in London 5 March, 1627, and that of his wife Elizabeth 4 March, 1638. Thomas left to his son Robert all his lands in Virginia. Descendants of this family are now living in Pennsylvania and New York.

FLEET. Lancaster county.

Arms: Chequy or and gules, a canton argent.

Capt. Henry Fleet, born about 1600, died about 1661, came to Virginia before 1623, at which date he was captured by the Indians and remained with them until 1627. He was Burgess for Lancaster in 1652. He was a merchant and trader and wrote "A brief journal of a voyage made in the bark 'Virginia,' to Virginia and the other parts of the Continent of America." His wife Sarah married after his death, Col. John Walker of Rappahannock, by whom she had several daughters. By Capt. Fleet, she had a son, Henry, died 1728, Justice of Lancaster in 1695, Sheriff in 1718 and 1719. He married Elizabeth Wildey, by whom he had: (1) Henry; (2) William; (3) Elizabeth; (4) Judith, married 1723, William Hobson of Northumberland; (5) Margaret, married Presley Cox of Westmoreland; (6) Ann, married Leonard Howson of Northumberland; (7) a daughter who married Brent.

The maternal ancestry of Capt. Henry Fleet is very distinguished. Sir Henry Wyatt of Allington Castle, Kent, Privy Councillor to Henry VIII., married Elizabeth, daughter of Thomas Brooke, Lord Cobham. Their son, Sir Thomas Wyatt, "The Rebel," born 1520, beheaded on Tower Hill, 11 April, 1554, married Jane, daughter of Sir William Howt. Their daughter Joan Wyatt, married Charles Scott, son of Sir Reginald Scott of Scott Hall, Kent, and their daughter, Deborah Scott, married William Fleet, gent., of Chatham, Kent, a member of the Virginia Company. They had issue, seven sons and four daughters; four of the sons being among the early immigrants to Virginia and Maryland, viz: (1) Henry; (2) Edward, member of the Maryland Legislature in 1638; (3) Reginold, member of the Maryland Legislature in 1638; (4) John, member of the Maryland Legislature in 1638.

TAYLOR. Caroline county.

Crest: A naked arm couped at the shoulder embowed, holding an arrow ppr.

Motto: Consequitur quodcunque petit.

James Taylor, ancestor of the Caroline county family of that name, is said to have come from the vicinity of Carlisle, England. He was in Virginia before 1650 and took out patents of land on the Mattaponi River. By his first wife, Frances, he had Jane, born 27 Dec., 1668; James, born 1674; Sarah, born 1676. His first wife died in 1680, and in 1682 he married Mary, sister of John Gregory, by whom he had the following children: John and Anne, twins, born 1685, John died young; Mary, born 1688; Edmund, born 1690; John, born 1693, died young; Elizabeth, born 1694, died young; John, born 1696. James Taylor died about 1698 at an advanced age. An old ring handed down in the family is said to have once been his property, and it bears engraved upon it the above crest which is that of the Taylors of Pennington Castle. The descendants of James Taylor have been exceedingly prominent in the history of the State, one of them—Zachary, becoming President.

BUCKNER. Gloucester county.

Arms: Sable three fleurs de lis or.

Crest: A fleur de lis gules, an adder entwined around it issuing from the centre leaf ppr.

John and Philip Buckner, brothers, were in Virginia as early as

1667, and possibly before that time. They were the sons of Thomas Buckner, who was baptized at Oxford in 1590, and grandsons of Hugh Buckner, who was Bailiff of Oxford in 1592. The family were originally of Cumnor in Berkshire. John Buckner patented land in Gloucester county in 1667, and in 1671 was a vestryman of Petsworth Parish, he was also Clerk of the County, and in 1683 a member of the House of Burgesses. He is noted as being the first man to introduce the printing press into Virginia. He died about 1695, as in that year there is an inventory of his estate recorded in Essex county. His wife's name is not known, but he had at least the following children: (1) William of York county; (2) John of Gloucester county; (3) Richard of Caroline county; (4) Thomas of Gloucester county; (5) Elizabeth, who married James Williams. Philip Buckner, brother of the first John, settled in Stafford county, and it is thought married Elizabeth Sadler in 1667. He died about 1699, as his will is probated in Stafford county in that year. He had issue ,two sons, Robert, who was alive in 1722, and Andrew.

WASHINGTON. Westmoreland county.

Arms: Argent two bars gules, in chief three mullets of the second.

Crests: (1) Out of a ducal coronet or, a raven wings endorsed ppr. (2) Out of a ducal coronet or, an eagle, wings endorsed sable.

That George Washington, President of the United States, was descended from Royalty can be shown by the following descent, commencing with Edward I., although the descent can be carried back for many more generations: (1) Edward I., King of England, married Margaret, daughter of Philip III., King of France; (2) Edmund of Woodstock, Earl of Kent, married Margaret, daughter of John, Lord Wake; (3) Sir Thomas Holland, died 1360, married Joan, "the fair maid of Kent"; (4) Thomas Holland, Earl of Kent, died 1397, married Alice, daughter of Richard, Earl of Arundel; (5) Eleanor, died 1405, married Edward Charlton, Baron Powis; (6) Sir John Tiptoft, died 1443, married Joyce Charlton, born 1403;(7) Edmond Sutton, married Joyce Tiptoft; (8) John Sutton, died 1487; (9) Sir John Sutton, living 1541, of Aston-le-Walls; (10) Margaret Sutton, heiress of Aston-le-Walls, buried there 17 April, 1563, married John Butler, buried 1558; (11) Alban Butler, buried at Aston-le-Walls, 27 April, 1609; (12) Simon Butler, married Barbara Washington, the daughter of Laurence Washington of Sulgrave. Barbara (Washington) Butler's brother, Robert Washington, married Elizabeth Light, by whom Laurence Washington of Sulgrave, buried at Brington 1616, who married 3 Aug., 1588, Margaret Butler, the daughter of William Butler of Tighes, Sussex, and the brother of Alban Butler, named above. (13) Laurence Washington, son of Laurence, was Rector of Purleigh, Essex, and expelled from the living in 1643, he married Amphyllis Rhodes. (14) John Washington, born 1631, died 1671, married Anna Pope and went to Virginia. (15) Laurence Washington mar-

ried Mildred Warner. (16) Augustine Washington married Mary
Ball. (17) George Washington, President.

The Washington family came to Virginia about 1657 and was
represented by John and his brother Laurence. The elder John
was employed against the Indians in Maryland, and as a reward
for his services was made "Colonel," and the parish where he lived
was named after him. He was baptised at Warton, Lancaster,
England, in 1627, and died in 1677, within a few days of his brother
Laurence. He was married first in England, but his wife and two
children died soon after arrival in Virginia. By his second wife,
Anne Pope, he had issue: Laurence, born about 1661; John, born
about 1663; Elizabeth, born about 1665; Anne, born about 1667.

UNDERHILL. York county.

Arms: Sable two bars argent, on a chief or a mount vert.

Capt. John Underhill of Felgates Creek, York county, was born in
the city of Worcester, England. He died 1672-3 and his tomb at
"Ringfield" has armorial bearings. They are too broken for posi-
tive identification, the "two bars" being distinguishable, however.
As Capt. Underhill was born in Worcester, and as there is but one
family of the name having "bars" in their arms, viz: Underhill of
Worcestershire, the above arms are undoubtedly correct. Capt.
Underhill's will was proved in York county, 24 Feb., 1672-3; mentions children, John, Nathaniel and Mary. To John he leaves the
plantation on Felgate's Creek, and to Nathaniel land in New Kent
county. Capt. Underhill married in 1660 Mary, widow of William
Felgate, skinner, of London, and brother of Capt. Robert Felgate.
The widow had another husband, Thomas Bassett, who left two
children, William and Mary. The former moved to New Kent,
where he patented lands jointly with Capt. Underhill.

FOLLIOTT. York county.

Arms: Argent a lion rampant, double queued purpure, crowned
or.

The Rev. Edward Folliott was minister of York Parish from
1652 to 1690. He left two daughters: (1) Elizabeth, who married,
first, Josias Moody, and, secondly, Capt. Charles Hansford; (2)
Mary, married first Dr. Henry Power, secondly, John Seal. There
are many descendants from the above two daughters. A pedigree
of the Folliott family is given in Nash's "History of Worcestershire." Francis Folliott married Avis, daughter of Thomas Tracey
of North Piddle, and had a son John, who married Eleanor, daughter and heir of John More of Dunclent, they had a son, Thomas
of Pirton, Worcestershire, who married Catherine, daughter of
Sir William Lygon of Madresfield, and they had a son John,
knighted in 1603, who married Elizabeth, daughter of John Aylmer,
Bishop of London. Sir John resided at Naunton, Worcestershire,
and had a son, Edward, born 1610, matriculated at Oxford, 1632,
who was Rector of Alderton, Northampton, until 1634, when the
living was sequestrated by the Parliamentary Committee. Rev.

Edward afterwards came to Virginia. Henry Folliott, brother of Sir John, was created in 1619, Baron Folliott of Ballyshannon, Ireland.

ROANE. Gloucester county.

Arms: Argent three stags trippant ppr.

Chest: A stag's head erased ppr, attired or, holding in the mouth an acorn of the last leaved vert.

Charles Roane came to Virginia as early as 1664, and settled in Gloucester county, his first patent for land being entered 13 Sept., 1664. He left at least one son, William Roane of Petsworth Parish, Gloucester county, who in 1726, bought land in Essex county, and was the ancestor of Judge Spencer Roane. Charles Roane was the son of Robert Roane of Chaldon, Surrey, gent., whose will was proved 5 May, 1676. In it he specifically mentions his son Charles of Virginia, as follows: "To son Charles Roane and to his child or children, if any, £600, and to discharge him and them of all sums paid for his use since his transport to Virginia. To his wife, Mrs. Frances Roane, £20. To his son, Robert Roane, £100, if his father be living." He also leaves his son Thomas the manor of Tollesworth in Surrey, and in default to his Charles in Virginia. Thomas Roane, brother of the immigrant, died in 1689, aged 39 years, and his tomb at Chaldon, Surrey, bears the above arms, impaling "3 falconers gloves" which are the arms of his wife Elizabeth, daughter of Henry Bartelot, who died in 1701, aged 30 years.

GILMER. Williamsburg.

Arms: Azure a chevron between two fleurs de lis in chief or, and a writing pen full feathered in base argent.

Dr. George Gilmer, son of William Gilmer, an advocate, was born near Edinburgh, Scotland, in 1700. He studied medicine at the University of Edinburgh and went to London to practice with Dr. Ridgway. He married the daughter of his partner and, in 1731, came to Williamsburg. He married 2nd, Mary Peachy, in 1732, daughter of Dr. Thomas Walker of King and Queen. By her he had two sons, Peachy Ridgway and George. He married 3rd, in 1745, Harrison Blair, sister of the Hon. John Blair, president of the Virginia Council. This last wife bore two sons—John and William —and died 1755. Dr. Gilmer died in Williamsburg, Jan. 15, 1755. The arms are taken from the Gilmer book-plate.

QUISENBERRY. Jamestown.

Arms: Escartele de or et de azur, au hon de sable arme et lampassee, de gules la queue fourchette brochant sur les escarteleurs. Casque couronne.

Crest: Un panache de cinque plumes de autriche, escartele de or et de azur.

Lambrequin: De or et de azur.

The Quisenberry family descend from Heinrich Questenburg of Cologne, Germany, who settled in Canterbury, England, in 1467.

A descendant, Thomas, settled near Jamestown about 1624. A branch of the family, John Quesenbury, settled in Northumberland county in 1649. An extended pedigree of the family is found "In the Memorials of the Quisenberry Family," published by A. C. Quisenberry, of Hyattsville, Md.

STRACHAN. Prince George county.

Arms: Azure a stag trippant or, attired and unguled gules, for Strachan. Argent a saltire sable on a chief of the second three oak leaves ppr. for Blackwood.

Dr. Alexander Glas Strachan, son of Joseph Strachan and Miss Glas, the granddaughter of Sir Robert Blackwood of Petrovia, Scotland, was born on the Strachan estates at Luscar, near Edinburgh, 29 July, 1748. He was educated in the latter city and came to Virginia, settling near Petersburg, and was vestryman for Bristol Parish 1785. He was descended from the ancient house of Strachan of Thornton. He married twice, and by his second wife, a Miss Field of Petersburg, had issue eight children, viz: Robert Glas Strachan, Theophilus Field Strachan, John Blackwood Strachan, Alexander Glas Strachan, Martha, Eliza, Jane and Mary Strachan. The family intermarried with the Fields, Bollings, Blands and Madisons.

WALDOE. Lancaster county.

Arms: Argent, a chevron between three birds sable, beaked and legged or.

The above arms are on a wax seal at Lancaster court-house, said impression being on the will of Edward Waldoe, dated 1693-4. The arms correspond with the English arms of Waldoure, which has in addition; for a crest, "a wolf's head erased or."

Index

Index